ALCIDAMAS

THE WORKS & FRAGMENTS

Edited with Introduction,
Translation and Commentary by
J.V. MUIR

Bristol Classical Press

Cover illustration: A miserable Palamedes in the Underworld,
watched over by a relaxed Persephone, detail from a red-figure *krater*
in the Metropolitan Museum of Art, New York [08.258.21]

Published in 2001 by
Bristol Classical Press
an imprint of
Gerald Duckworth & Co. Ltd
61 Frith Street
London W1D 3JL
e-mail: inquiries@duckworth-publishers.co.uk
Website: www.ducknet.co.uk

Reprinted 2002

A catalogue record for this book is available
from the British Library

ISBN 1-85399-610-6

Typesetting by J.V. Muir

Printed in Great Britain by
Antony Rowe Ltd, Eastbourne

Contents

Preface   iv

Introduction
    Alcidamas' life   v
    Context of Alcidamas' work   vii
    Alcidamas' works   xiii
    Alcidamas' style   xxi
    The Text   xxii

Notes to Introduction   xxiii

Select Bibliography   xxx

List of Abbreviations   xxxiii

Text   1

Commentary   40

General Index   93

Index of Greek Words   94

Preface

This edition of Alcidamas is chiefly intended to make more easily available two short texts which are, I believe, not without interest. They come from a formative period of Greek rhetoric for which there is not that much evidence, and in recent times they have only been accessible in Radermacher's *Artium Scriptores* or Avezzù's largely textual Italian edition. The treatise *On those who write written speeches* certainly deserves a wider readership, for it says some vivid and sensible things about public speaking and there is nothing quite like it in the surviving literature of the period.

Many friends have helped. Professor Pat Easterling and Professor Malcolm Willcock looked at my original suggestions and gave helpful advice and much encouragement (as they have done to so many others); Professor Easterling in particular located an elusive dissertation at a crucial moment. I have done much of the work in the Joint Library of the Hellenic and Roman Societies at the Institute of Classical Studies, and I should to thank Professor Waywell and the staff there for their unfailing efficiency and for the atmosphere of quiet hospitality which makes the Library such a pleasant place in which to read. I should also like to thank John Betts, Graham Douglas and Jean Scott of the Bristol Classical Press for much perceptive comment and for the very detailed help they gave with many technical matters -- helpful and kindly taskmasters. My best thanks, however, go to my erstwhile colleague, Dr. Mike Trapp of the Department of Classics at King's College London; he read a draft of the edition at a very busy time and sent back a host of comments and suggestions which saved me from many crude mistakes and greatly improved both the translation and the commentary. He has rare gifts, and any who know his scholarship (or his teaching) will appreciate the advantages I have enjoyed. For the errors and misjudgements which remain I am wholly responsible and offer my apologies.

Introduction

Alcidamas' life

Alcidamas was born on the edge of the Greek world in Asia Minor, probably during the last quarter of the fifth century BC. His father, Diocles, was said to have been a writer of *mousika*, but nothing is known of the family circumstances. His birthplace, Elaia, was a small town on the coast of Mysia which served as the port of Pergamon and consequently became more prominent later under the Attalids; it had probably been one of the original members of the Delian Confederacy and was a regular, if small, subscriber.[1] How Alcidamas rose from his small-town beginnings is not known, but he became a pupil of the famous teacher of rhetoric and sophist, Gorgias, and he and Isocrates were the two best-known rhetoricians to emerge from among the sophist's students; he was probably a little older than Isocrates.[2] There is some evidence of a close and none-too-friendly rivalry between Alcidamas and Isocrates, stemming in part from fundamental differences on how rhetoric should be taught and practised, Alcidamas representing the professional, vocational teacher responding to the needs of the customer whilst Isocrates made rather more lofty claims.[3] The matter and manner of *On those who write written speeches* (henceforth *OWS*) strongly suggest that Alcidamas worked primarily as a teacher, but, like his mentor and unlike his rival, he appears to have had serious interests in other directions too; whatever it contained, his book, the *Mouseion*, was probably not a technical work on the art of speaking. He was quite an influential figure in his day: Aeschines was said to have been his pupil, Demosthenes studied his work,[4] and although Aristotle quotes him in Book iii of the *Rhetoric* in order to criticise his style (along with Gorgias and Lykophron), he clearly took his writings seriously.[5] After Gorgias' death Alcidamas is said to have taken over his 'school', but whether this refers to a group of pupils or the continuance of Gorgias' methods of teaching is not clear.[6] He was probably active as a teacher from the end of the fifth century BC and his 'Messenian Speech' may give a terminus for surviving works around 369 BC. Like many sophists and teachers of rhetoric he probably travelled a good deal between the larger Greek cities, but his evident rivalry with Isocrates, his familiarity with the ideas of Socrates/Plato and his role as Aeschines' teacher suggest that he spent some considerable time in Athens. He had a small place in the technical history of rhetoric, being remembered as the author of one of the basic classifications of language – into assertion, denial, question and address.[7] Cicero had read Alcidamas' *Encomium of Death* and, although he politely pointed out shortcomings in philosophical technicalities, he admired Alcidamas' *ubertas* and described him as *rhetor antiquus in primis nobilis*.[8] The author of [Plut.] *De lib. educ.* 6F had read *OWS*, and he remembered and used the vivid image of the chained prisoners who are released but are still creatures of habit (§17). Quintilian mentions Alcidamas among those who had written rhetorical handbooks, and he also says that Plato refers to 'Alcidamas Elaites' as Palamedes (which looks like a reference to Plato, *Phaedrus* 261d).[9] The speeches of Alcidamas still seem to have been available to and read by John Tzetzes in the twelfth century AD.[10] In contexts other than rhetoric, Alcidamas is quoted by the Hadrianic compiler/editor of the *Contest between Homer and Hesiod* as the source for one version of the death of Hesiod's murderers,[11] and a scholiast refers to Alcidamas' followers debating views on Stoic philosophy.[12] It has been suggested that, quite apart from any embryo stylistic awareness to be found in *OWS*, Alcidamas was also interested in literary discussion and comment: his memorable description of the *Odyssey* as 'a fine mirror of human life' is often quoted, and the other phrases which Aristotle gives in *Rhetoric* iii may possibly belong to a work of literary discussion.[13] There is also an intriguing hint that Alcidamas may have written the lives of some of the Pre-Socratic philosophers, including Zeno and Empedocles, in a book entitled the *Physikon*.[14]

All in all, the picture emerges of someone who, whilst not intellectually in the first rank, was yet interesting enough to be accepted by contemporaries as one of the more serious figures in a new and developing discipline in the first quarter of the fourth century BC, who was a part of the cultural milieu and probably more than a narrow technician and teacher, and who was reckoned by later antiquity to have earned his place in the early history of rhetoric, not just by his reflections on the nature of speech-making but by the examples of his work which still survived and were read.

The context of Alcidamas' work

According to Cicero and the tradition, Greek rhetoric had its origins in Sicily; the two Syracusans, Corax and Tisias, were said to have devised the first elements of the art because the expulsion of the tyrants from some of the Sicilian cities (e.g. Thrasydaeus from Acragas in 472 BC and Thrasybulus from Syracuse in 466) had led to a number of law-suits in which citizens tried to recover their property; they needed help.[15] Corax and Tisias are shadowy figures; they probably worked in the first half of the fifth century BC but their exact dates and precise contributions are unknown, and there are quite good grounds for supposing that the ancient tendency to credit founding fathers with later developments was healthily at work in their case.[16] Gorgias, the great sophist and teacher of rhetoric, was said to have been one of their pupils. Athens too had a 'foundation legend' to explain the sudden burgeoning of rhetoric, and this was based upon Gorgias' visit to the city in 427 BC as a representative of his native Sicilian city, Leontinoi; the speech or speeches he made on this occasion are said to have made a dramatic impression and to have given the impetus to the use and teaching of rhetoric at Athens. Thucydides mentions the visit of the delegation (not Gorgias himself), but there are good reasons for believing that there was no such sudden start and that the story at Athens goes back much further.[17] Gorgias may well have made a successful and effective appearance in 427 BC, but at that date formal speech-making can hardly have been a novelty. Gorgias himself would have been sixty and towards the end of his active career, and Protagoras, Hippias and Antiphon had all been teaching or practising the art for some time. Little is known about the detailed activities of Protagoras or Hippias in rhetoric, but Antiphon would have been in his fifties in 427 BC and his surviving works suggest a considerable figure in the development of rhetorical practice and education.[18] The three sets of four speeches by him known as the *Tetralogies* (two speeches for the prosecution and two for the defence in each set) contain short pieces only and are plainly meant as instructional material. On the other hand the three surviving court-room speeches which Antiphon wrote obviously derive from the real thing – full-scale works, closely argued and very accomplished in dealing with legal technicalities, and they justify the admiration which Thucydides expresses for their author; they are hardly first attempts at a new art.[19] Antiphon did not restrict his activity to writing for the courts and teaching, but also took a dangerous part in politics, and fragments of two of his speeches to the Athenian Assembly are extant. These interests point to the two characteristic aims of early rhetorical education: vocational training for public speaking in the courts or in politics (or in both).[20] This in turn indicates a more realistic stimulus for the early growth of rhetoric at Athens than the spectacular appearance of a well-known performer.[21] In public life there is no doubt that the growth of democracy following the reforms of Cleisthenes and Ephialtes in time resulted in a situation in which anyone who wished for a part – large or small – in political decision-making needed to pay attention to the arts of persuasion and effective speaking. During the second half of the fifth century BC the *ekklesia* decided all significant state and legal affairs at Athens, and the skill of swaying large meetings became indispensable for would-be leaders of opinion. Likewise Ephialtes' transfer of much legal jurisdiction from the Areopagus to the jury-courts in 462–1 BC helped to produce a remarkable growth in legal activity, often involving the ordinary citizen, and this continued to the point where Athenians were laughing at themselves for having such a litigious society.[22] Laughter aside, any citizen could find himself arguing before arbitrators or making a speech in his own cause before a very large and not always very attentive jury; he too needed help. From the last quarter of the fifth century BC there was a lively and growing market for both speech-writers and for instruction in public speaking, and there is evidence for pretty keen competition among the practitioners together with strenuous efforts to retain a loyal following of students.[23] The composition of speeches was becoming thoroughly commercialized in the person of the *logographos* who, following in the steps of Antiphon, wrote court-room speeches for particular occasions and customers to order and for pay – his efforts were commonly employed well into the fourth century even though they must often have been rather hard for the ordinary citizen to use effectively.[24] For all that his role may sometimes have extended beyond plain speech-writer – even to being used as a kind of legal consultant[25] – the *logographos* was not very highly regarded: Isocrates had had to write speeches for clients in his early years in order to make a living (Aristotle rather cattily said that bundles of them could be had at shops in the Agora[26]), but he preferred to forget this aspect of his past and regarded speeches for ordinary court-room proceedings with some disdain.[27] The practice of the logographers naturally tended to a degree of systematization, a part of which may have been inherited from the Sicilian tradition, and simple didactic outlines and procedures began to emerge. The evolution of speech-structure, for instance, clearly came early and had obvious advantages: it gave speakers a pattern for construction, and it gave juries some expectation of shape and order in what was otherwise a rather loose legal process. There has been some scepticism about the production of even simple rhetorical manuals with advice on such things as structure before the end of the fifth century BC, and it has been suggested that model speeches rather than manuals were the usual patterns for teaching (the word *techne* being at first used for such a model speech).[28] Aristotle later certainly had hard things to say about Gorgias and other early teachers who relied on model speeches in their courses of instruction: it was, he said, like teaching an apprentice to make shoes by simply showing him a pair ready-made.[29] However, Plato, *Phaedrus* 266d–267d sketches a recognisable outline of classic speech-structure associating it with the names of early rhetoricians including Tisias, and it seems reasonable to think that some teaching of systematic construction and types of argument was a part of early rhetorical training. Certainly, when Aristotle came to make his celebrated collection of rhetorical manuals, he seems to have found no lack of them.[30]

The last quarter of the fifth century BC and the earlier years of the fourth before Aristotle's influential systematization of rhetoric, were times of experiment when the technical vocabulary and elementary structures of rhetoric were evolving; attention was being given to all those things which later became the classic components of the art. There were experiments with formal structure (Antiphon and Lysias especially), with style and methods of developing material (Gorgias, Isocrates, Polus and Antisthenes), with types of proof and argument (Antiphon and some of the practices lampooned in Aristophanes' *Clouds* – a development by no means confined to rhetoric; cf. the *Dissoi Logoi*), with the training of memory (Alcidamas, Theodectes),[31] and with delivery and the ways in which a speaker could 'hold' an audience (Alcidamas especially). In the fully developed Roman system of rhetoric, these would be called *dispositio, elocutio, inventio, memoria* and *actio*, and it is with the last of these that Alcidamas' treatise is primarily concerned. The problem of making contact with one's hearers was particularly acute for Athenians since the two typical contexts for formal speeches – the courts and the Assembly – involved speaking to large audiences running into hundreds or even thousands. There are two extremes in such circumstances: on the one hand, the speaker who can feel and stir the emotions of a mass audience by forming a 'live' relationship with them, adjusting his words accordingly; on the other, the speaker with a text in written rather than spoken register who is bound to it and recites the words, but makes scarcely any real contact with those listening.

The early history of rhetoric is sometimes treated in isolation as if composition and speech-making were special, suddenly-developed skills. In fact the experience of hearing carefully and elaborately composed speeches was to be had in Athens in contexts other than politics or the courts far earlier than Gorgias' supposedly ground-breaking visit in 427 BC. The particularly Athenian custom of the *epitaphios*, the public speech in honour of those who had died in battle for the city, goes back at least to the decade 470–460 BC, and probably even to the Persian Wars.[32] There were the Homeric recitations – and the speeches in Homer are often far from artless[33] – and the plays at the Great Dionysia had accustomed large audiences of citizens to the speech as a crafted, scripted performance. In addition the travelling virtuosos like Gorgias and Hippias with their costumes and sense of performance had created an eager – often young – audience for the speech as an artistic recital; they were to be heard on their visits to cities, on public occasions, and as star turns at some of the great festivals.[34] As Isocrates later observed, such public events were ideal for the orator who wanted to put himself about.[35] However, the speech delivered for display or entertainment in the recital room or on the festival platform represented a significant change of purpose: the medium was becoming the message, and as a consequence the message soon became deliberately trivial – bumble-bees or salt, as Isocrates tartly observed.[36] Such events relied on the skill of the orator or the rhapsode or the actor in front of an audience, but, with the possible exceptions of the *epitaphios* and the festival performance, they ultimately depended on a text which had been carefully composed by an author, and which was then studied, learnt and performed. This mirrored the situation in which many Athenians found themselves when they sought professional help from a *logographos*. The examples of logographers' speeches which we possess were probably prepared carefully for publication, but what an ancient customer received from a logographer was undoubtedly the script of a speech prepared and written to a commission; the problem was how to use it convincingly, whether it was read or, more likely, delivered from memory. The skilled professional performer on stage or at a recital could recreate a memorized text, establish a relationship with an audience and present the illusion of living language,[37] but, if an unskilled amateur with all the pressures of a law-court or a political meeting was trying to use *verbatim* a script written by someone else, the result was all too likely to be flat, dull and hesitant. Such public failure could damage both the self-esteem of the speaker (not a negligible factor in the Greek world) and the effectiveness of his plea. The avoidance of such embarrassment and the methods of making cogent arguments by establishing real audience-contact are essentially the subjects of Alcidamas' treatise and the scorn which he pours on the text-bound orator strongly reinforces the view that the appearance, at any rate, of direct, spontaneous communication was vital to anyone who needed to command a large audience either in the courts or in the Assembly.[38]

How then was a written text normally used in the delivery of a speech ? It is usually accepted that Antiphon was the first to have a written text for a court-room speech when he appeared in his own defence after his political adventures in 411 BC, but this landmark is suspect since the tradition itself is confused.[39] What it presumably means is that he actually had his text with him as a reminder (on a set of writing tablets ?, on unnumbered papyrus sheets ?, on a papyrus roll ? – none of these was very user-friendly for the speaker), and that this became more common. The usual practice was probably what it still was in Plato's day: in the *Phaedrus* a young student has the text of a speech, memorizes it and performs it, and the speech may also serve as a model for discussion or imitation.[40] For Demosthenes too the norm for the court-room or political speaker was clearly delivery from a composed text committed to memory; forgetting one's lines was as bad for the orator as for the actor.[41] Alcidamas saw the dangers and limitations of the text-based speaker – even a text-based speaker performing from memory – very clearly and from obvious personal experience. He knew that, although the ambitious politician in the Assembly or the *Boule* might fancy himself a second Gorgias, such a person also had to be flexible and sensitive enough to adjust to the moods of a large, unpredictable audience and adaptable enough to seize whatever opportunity – or *kairos* as Gorgias would have put it – that circumstances presented to him. Likewise the law-court speaker could never know precisely what the other side was going to say and he too needed adaptability. Gorgias' extraordinary talents had been able to encompass the requirements of both striking improvisation and elaborately constructed speeches, but such virtuosity was not available to all.[42]

Alcidamas, in championing improvisation, is clearly conscious that he adopting a defensive position in a changing world and that he has big battalions against him. The written composition of legal, political and artistic speeches had the cachet of being associated with conspicuous public events and professional performers, and it also had the advantage that it could be systematized and codified, and – in its cruder forms – taught to the uninitiated at quite simple levels and with quite simple models. Antiphon's *Tetralogies* and the extant speeches of Gorgias with their saturation-teaching techniques in such things as antithesis and parison (parallelism of structure) are obvious examples. On the other side, impromptu fluency, however useful, was much more difficult to grasp, for it was harder to teach and the results were unpredictable; an inexperienced speaker was likely to prefer the security of a prepared text which could be memorized *verbatim*, while, for those on the supply side, the text was a tangible, marketable commodity. Alcidamas is very aware of these tendencies, and doubtless that is why he too published display speeches for advertisement or performance; the four known *encomia* (*On Death*, *On Poverty*, *On Nais* and *On Proteus the dog*) seem to fit into this mould. Nevertheless, his reasonable conviction seems to have remained that 'live', responsive communication and a real relationship with an audience was the most effective way of making a public speech. His chief rival, Isocrates, though not unaware of the issues Alcidamas raised, much preferred composition in the study and, for instance spent at least ten years polishing the *Panegyrikos*.[43]

Such was the context in which the function of the written text in the self-conscious 'speech' was debated and finally established, the context in which Alcidamas, Isocrates and their contemporaries worked and taught. Isocrates in latter years took only a small number of very gifted pupils with whom he worked intensively – perhaps as few as six.[44] He taught rhetoric as a cultivated art, but he claimed to be teaching more than a vocational skill and reckoned to educate his pupils towards *philosophia* (though he did not mean by that what Plato meant).[45] We know nothing of Alcidamas' methods of teaching, but *OWS* and the *Odysseus* are plainly directed at those using rhetoric in the law and political life (and at those who wished to teach them) rather than a few individuals in a 'philosophical' tutorial, and the kind of speaking envisaged is neither educational nor an art-form but a persuasive means to a defined end.[46]

Alcidamas' works

On those who write written speeches *or* On sophists

The main purpose of *OWS* is clear: it is intended to convince the reader that an improvised, adaptable speech, tailored to the needs of the occasion and the mood of the audience is much to be preferred to a speech delivered from and limited by a text – and by implication, perhaps, to persuade the reader also that a course of instruction leading to that end is a good investment. It is, however, by no means obvious exactly what the treatise is in terms of literary form. The secondary title *On sophists* invites comparison with the 'speech' of Isocrates entitled *Against the sophists*, but *OWS* is certainly not a formal speech, even if the tone is that of the persuader, and in any case Isocrates' piece can hardly be called a speech either. There is no sign in *OWS* of even the simplest conventional speech-structure other than a loose introduction and a concluding paragraph, and there is no form of address to a real or imaginary audience (Alcidamas' claim to be making an accusation – *kategoria* – in §1 does not classify the work). The purpose appears to be didactic, but what is given is not actual teaching, e.g. how to prepare yourself for extempore speaking, but rather a programme of what should be taught and arguments for its importance; it is designed to attract and persuade and to whet the appetite. Modern writers have been cautious and non-committal in their description of the nature of the work, but from what Alcidamas himself says in §31, it is possible that *OWS* is something rather unusual: the only example we have of how an early fourth century BC rhetor advertised part of his wares, giving a kind of public prospectus for a course of instruction.[47] Ideally, Alcidamas would be addressing an audience of prospective students and doubtless following his own precepts by tailoring his words to the mood of the moment, but for those who could not be there, the skilful, publicity-conscious rhetor was not averse to using information technology – the written word – second-best though he might consider it to be. It has been suggested that *OWS* is only a part of a larger work and that it is in fact the preface to Alcidamas' much discussed *Mouseion*.[48] This is surely wrong; if the *Mouseion* was, as seems possible, a miscellany of writing about famous literary figures, *OWS* would be a very weird prologue, giving no hint of what it purported to introduce. Moreover, its concluding paragraph is quite clearly a conclusion, not simply an interim summing–up.

The rhetorical background to the treatise is what might be expected from a pupil of Gorgias, with some notable additions and omissions. The main thrust of the argument in favour of extempore speaking is not surprising in someone taught by a brilliant improviser. Likewise, the doctrine of the 'critical moment' (*kairos*) on which Gorgias seems to have laid some emphasis is quite prominent in Alcidamas. The techniques of expanding and abbreviating subject-matter (*makrologia* and *brachylogia*) for which Gorgias was known are referred to by Alcidamas as well as the idea of 'what is fitting' (*to prepon*). Structure (*taxis*) too is mentioned but with no kind of elaboration, and some words are becoming semi-technical like 'precision of style' (*akribeia* or *akribeiai*). Strangely absent are examples of that repetitive patterning of phrase-structure and argument which makes the fragment from Gorgias' *Epitaphios* such a favourite quote with stylistic critics (apart from one reference to rhythm in §16). Relationships with fellow professionals are not cordial; there is the general assault on the credentials of rival teachers at the start and undoubted signs of friction with Isocrates. Perhaps the most surprising evidence of a connection is with Plato/Socrates: Alcidamas had clearly picked up some notion of the theory of Forms and had also read at least the last section of the *Phaedrus* where the mythical story of Theuth is taken up by Socrates to expand on the limitations of the written word.

Much has been written to try to reconstruct an orderly public exchange of views between Alcidamas and Isocrates, and to locate *OWS* within such an exchange.[49] The two men were Gorgias' star pupils, successful teachers themselves and of very different opinions, and rivalry is clear to see. It has been suggested that *OWS* is a public answer to Isocrates' *Against the sophists* but it has also been quite cogently argued that the reverse is the case too; certainty is impossible. It is true that coincidences of vocabulary and difference of viewpoint on the same topics give evidence of point-scoring between the two men, but the evidence does not fall into an obvious pattern of point and counter-point. We are hearing sharp voices in a running argument and Avezzù and others have suggested a sequence involving other works of Isocrates and have attempted to date the sequence :–

Before 390 BC	Isoc. *Helen*
c. 390 BC	Alcid. *OWS*
c. 390 BC	Isoc. *Against the sophists*
389/5 – 380 BC	Isoc. *Panegyrikos*

However, such attempts lie in the realm of speculation.

Against the treachery of Palamedes

This is an imaginary prosecution-speech delivered by Odysseus in front of the Greek army at Troy in which he accuses his fellow-soldier, Palamedes, of treachery. In spirit and manner it belongs to the law-courts, though there is some attempt to present an 'authentic' Homeric setting. In fact, the traditional story of Palamedes' treachery does not occur in the *Odyssey* or the *Iliad* but derives from the *Cypria*.[50] Odysseus and Palamedes had fallen out before the Trojan War; when the Greek force was being assembled, Odysseus had tried to avoid the draft on grounds of psychological disturbance (he was sowing his fields with sea-salt to prove it), but Palamedes had shown him up by threatening the life of his baby son, Telemachus, thereby forcing Odysseus to demonstrate his mettle and his sanity. According to this version of the story, Odysseus took revenge when they got to Troy by getting a Trojan prisoner to write a fake letter from Priam to Palamedes in which a certain sum of gold was promised to Palamedes in return for betraying the Greeks; the precise sum was then buried in Palamedes' tent by Odysseus and the letter was 'accidentally' disclosed to Agamemnon. The gold was found and Palamedes was condemned by the army to be stoned to death. Palamedes' father, Nauplios, later took revenge for his son's death by encouraging some of the wives of the Greek warriors to have affaires during their husbands' absence, and by wrecking the returning Greek fleet at Cape Kaphareus in Euboea after making false beacon fires. Alcidamas has a rather different version of the story in which the main evidence for Palamedes' treachery is not the 'planted' gold, but an arrow shot from the Trojan side with a message from Paris written on it which promises 'all that you agreed with Telephos' and that Cassandra would be given to Palamedes as his wife. There is also the mysterious spear which Palamedes threw towards the Trojans which was retrieved by one of them, and which was also presumed to be carrying a message. There is no way of telling whether this version is Alcidamas' own invention but it does not occur elsewhere and the story of the 'planted' gold would have been a much less suitable subject for an imaginary speech: a manifestly duplicitous Odysseus leading for the prosecution would hardly have been satisfactory and the situation would not have presented a useful pattern for a typical legal problem.[51]

The speech is probably intended to serve the purposes of both display (an *epideixis*) and teaching, and it invites obvious comparison with the speech attributed to Gorgias in which Palamedes mounts an imaginary defence against the charges levelled at him. Both use the device of epic subject-matter as a neutral ground for the presentation of rhetorical paradigms, but the two speeches are quite differently targeted. Gorgias' *Palamedes* is an exercise in stylistics and types of argument, with familiar figures like antithesis much in evidence and a rather artificial assemblage of probability (or in this case *im*probability) arguments. Alcidamas' speech on the other hand, whilst containing many of the conventions, is an exemplar for dealing with a certain type of law-court situation, one in which the circumstantial evidence for the prosecution is quite good but the material piece of evidence which would have clinched the matter (in this case, the arrow) is missing. What is needed to tip the balance is therefore an effective attack on the character and reliability of the defendant. Accordingly, after the narrative and two rather flimsy pieces of circumstantial evidence, Alcidamas leads off with family history and demonstrates with a piece of quite racy narrative (complete with audience prompt – 'So, what happens next ?') that Palamedes comes from bad stock (it can hardly be denied that this part of the speech gets out of hand; the stories go on too long and the links with the accused become tenuous). Alcidamas then attacks Palamedes' personal standards and moral courage by pointing to his failure to protest and take action when Helen was seduced and abducted from Sparta. Palamedes' duplicity and susceptibility to bribes are established by his deliberate failure on the recruiting expedition to Chios and Cyprus, and his vanity and untruthfulness are revealed by his false claims to being a prolific inventor. The speech is rounded off with a short epilogue in which the familiar formula of 'everyone else will do it unless you convict' is used.

As a work of literature the speech is no rival to the best of Demosthenes or even to the much-praised lucidity of Lysias, but it does not altogether deserve some of the harsh things which have been said about it.[52] It offers a useful pattern for the clear presentation of the facts; it demonstrates the open admission of the lack of crucial evidence, placing it judiciously and explaining it in a favourable context; and it contains a fair sample of desirable ingredients for a successful character-assassination: unsavoury family background, inaction and implied cowardice in the face of obvious wrong-doing, manifest selfishness and corruption in important public affairs, and pathological intellectual dishonesty. It is reasonable to suppose that Alcidamas used this and other similar texts with students as examples and patterns from which 'live' speeches could be generated on real or imaginary themes; it is probably the kind of thing on which many young Greeks cut their teeth when they enrolled to improve their public speaking.

The authenticity of the speech has been doubted, and dates have been ascribed to it from the fourth to the second century BC; it has also been staunchly defended.[53] It must be admitted that the stylistic case for believing that the speech is not by the same author as *OWS* is very strong. There are quirks of style which any reader of *OWS* will notice e.g. a fondness for negatived or double-negatived adjectives and adverbs, a tendency to prefer abstract nouns, and a persistent clumsiness of sentence construction. These occur much less frequently in the *Odysseus* and it is quite hard to believe that a writer could simply divest himself of such ingrained habits. The case is strong, but not, I believe, conclusive. It would be, if the two works belonged to the same genre and were therefore directly comparable, but *OWS* is quite different in character to the *Odysseus*. The message in *OWS* is all-important and the writer hardly seems to care about the medium, whereas in the *Odysseus* he observes rhetorical and stylistic convention and is on his best behaviour. *OWS* is a treatise which falls into no defined literary category, whereas the *Odysseus* closely follows the pattern of a court-room prosecution speech. In these circumstances, stylistic discrepancy is hardly surprising. I believe that a number of small clues may tip the balance in favour of Alcidamas' authorship. First, the attribution of the speech to him clearly goes back as far as Quintilian who believed (probably wrongly) that Plato was thinking of Alcidamas in the *Phaedrus* when he referred to the 'Eleatic Palamedes'; the identification has no point unless Quintilian associated Alcidamas with a known work in which Palamedes was prominent.[54] Second, Palamedes' family background in the *Odysseus* threatens to get out of hand precisely because it strays too far into what would be familiar local stories for someone from Elaia, and the unnecessary mention of Menestheus, whilst no doubt pleasing to an Athenian audience, would also be understandable for someone who regarded Menestheus as the founder of his birthplace.[55] The author of the *Odysseus* is aware of the technicalities of minting coins and there is a likely echo of this in *OWS* too; likewise musical metaphors occur in both works.[56] None of these points is conclusive and an element of legitimate doubt remains, but I believe it is not unreasonable to suppose that *OWS* and the *Odysseus* were both written by Alcidamas.

Other works

Of Alcidamas' speeches, the *Messenian Speech* is twice referred to by Aristotle as if it were a well-known piece; two quotations survive.[57] The historical context for the speech is the Spartan defeat at Leuktra and the liberation of Messenia in 370–69 BC, but there is no way of knowing whether Alcidamas was specially invited to deliver a celebratory oration at a victory celebration or whether he simply composed the speech as a *jeu d'esprit*. Four praise-speeches are attested: an *Encomium of Death* (which Cicero had read), an *Encomium of Nais* (a *hetaira*), an *Encomium of Proteus the dog*, and an *Encomium of Poverty*.[58] Paradoxical topics like these became favourites for speeches written for display, the subject-matter being less important than the virtuosity of the rhetoric.

The case for some technical writing on rhetoric cannot be discounted though no titles are known and the evidence is late. Quintilian includes Alcidamas among those who wrote manuals, and the four-fold classification of language quoted by Diogenes Laertius would certainly fit into such a technical context. In addition, Dionysius of Halicarnassus includes Alcidamas with Theodorus, Thrasymachus, Antiphon, Isocrates and Anaximenes as 'writers of technical instructions'.[59]

The *Physikon* (Book of Nature) is mentioned only once as the context for Alcidamas' writings about Zeno and Empedocles; there is no reason to doubt that he did write a book of that name and, if he was identifying the teachers of two scientific thinkers, he was probably writing about them from a biographical point of view.[60]

Alcidamas also wrote a book entitled the *Mouseion*, and it is curious that more has been written about this in modern times than about Alcidamas' surviving works, even though its nature and contents are unknown. Speculation and controversy originated with two brilliant articles by the young Friedrich Nietzsche in which he argued that the strange work we know as the *Contest between Homer and Hesiod* was originally devised by Alcidamas and formed part of the *Mouseion;*[61] this appeared to receive confirmation from two subsequent publications of papyri.[62] Since then the *Mouseion* has been credited with various contents: it has been thought to be a large-scale work of literary history with a preface on poetry and its psychological effects, 'a compilation of varied learned material', a work in sections including one on Homer and probably a version of the *Contest*, a philosophical work with *OWS* as its preface, a source-book of material for orators, and a rhetorical textbook.[63] Discussion has centred not so much upon the overall content of the *Mouseion* as upon the idea that a version of the *Contest* (which in the complete form we possess is certainly of Hadrianic date)[64] was composed by Alcidamas and formed part of the *Mouseion* or, if not originally composed by him, was certainly included in that work. The argument rests on several facts: first, Stobaeus quotes a couplet of verses from the *Mouseion* which are found both in the Hadrianic version of the *Contest* and in a third century BC papyrus which contains a similar, but by no means identical, version of lines 70–101 of the *Contest;*[65] second, the compiler of the Hadrianic *Contest* quotes Alcidamas as the source for one version of the death of Hesiod's murderers;[66] finally, a second or early third century AD papyrus has some lines which are similar to the end of the Hadrianic *Contest* and are followed by some more personal closing lines which advertise the author's literary ambition and express gratitude to Homer for the pleasure he has given to everyone.[67] The papyrus text has a *subscriptio* reading 'Alci]damas: On Homer', and lines 15–25 certainly sound like the Alcidamas of *OWS*.[68] Nietzsche's proposals (or versions of them) appear to encompass the later evidence of the two papyri and have gained considerable acceptance. However, there are quite legitimate doubts: the two lines quoted by Stobaeus are also found in Theognis and elsewhere and, though Alcidamas may have used them in the *Mouseion*, he need not be the author nor would it necessarily follow that their occurrence in the *Contest* proves that work to have been part of the *Mouseion*; then again, the fact that the Hadrianic *Contest* quotes Alcidamas as the authority for one story about the death of Hesiod's murderers appears to distance Alcidamas from the work rather than the reverse; finally, a comparison of the third century BC papyrus version of the *Contest* with the Hadrianic version shows quite noticeable differences of wording in the linking passages between the quotations from Homer and Hesiod though the sense remains the same. A comparison of the third/fourth century AD Michigan papyrus with the end of the Hadrianic *Contest* reveals a very similar discrepancy. If the compiler of the *Contest* was using Alcidamas' work on Homer as he had used him in the case of Hesiod's murderers, the changes are easily explicable, and so is the omission of the more personal signing-off in lines 15–25 of the Michigan papyrus. I believe that the following may be safely said: first, that the compiler of the *Contest* (and a re-write – probably in the time of Hadrian – is almost certain) used Alcidamas as a source, that the couplet quoted by Stobaeus occurred in the *Mouseion*, that Alcidamas wrote either a section of the *Mouseion* or a separate book which dealt with Homer and that part of this too was used in the *Contest*. I have therefore printed only the couplet quoted by Stobaeus and the text of the Michigan papyrus; the case for the *Contest* being originally written by Alcidamas has, I think, still to be proved.

This leaves the likely nature of the *Mouseion* unclear. The word *mouseion* usually seems to have a sense of place – a spot connected with the Muses – but it also seems to be used for a collection; Polus, another pupil of Gorgias, had made *mouseia* of examples of different kinds of style.[69] The Michigan papyrus attests to biographical writing and possibly literary comment on Homer, and the *Contest* to biographical writing on Hesiod. If these were part of the *Mouseion*, then it may have been a collection of loosely biographical and literary essays on famous literary figures with verse quotations. This leaves open the possibility that Solmsen's speculative reconstruction may be broadly on the right lines. It may then be that Alcidamas' *Physikon* was a parallel work in which famous philosophers and scientific speculators were given similar treatment.

Alcidamas' style

It is not easy to write of Alcidamas' style since the two surviving examples of
any substance were written for different purposes and show marked stylistic
differences.[70] Moreover, Aristotle's criticisms of features of Alcidamas' style
are by no means those that seem obvious to us, and are not that easy to apply
to the two works we possess. Much has been made of Alcidamas' tendency
to use abstract nouns to a marked degree, and this is indeed a noticeable
feature of his writing. Certain patterns can be seen: e.g. abstracts often occur
as subjects of verbs of action (the same pattern can be found at about the same
frequency in the speeches of Thucydides); they also commonly occur in
phrases where the abstract noun is joined with words denoting some kind of
mental activity.[71] This marked use of abstract nouns is, however, a stylistic
trait not peculiar to Alcidamas at this period – Antiphon and Thucydides
certainly share it.[72] Alcidamas also has an orator's tendency to pleonasm, and
it is not hard to find phrases which may have been euphonious to hear but
contain redundancies.[73] He is also attracted to what seemed to Aristotle
unduly poetic and artificial language. He was fond of what seem to be
unusual words, though these occur for the most part in *OWS* [74] – neologism
is often a feature of technical writing in new disciplines. In all these respects
he may well be showing the influence of his teacher, Gorgias. Aristotle
criticised Alcidamas' use of metaphor, and this is puzzling, for, if stylistic
virtues were sought for in Alcidamas, a modern reader would probably
commend his vivid metaphors (e.g. the image of the released prisoners for the
effects of stylistic habit-forming, the idea of extempore speech as something
living and animate). Clumsiness and awkwardness in sentence construction is
certainly a charge which can be levelled, though much more in *OWS* than in
the *Odysseus*.[75] In choice of vocabulary Alcidamas has a strange quirk of
preference for double-negatived adjectives and adverbs, though this is not at
all a feature of the *Odysseus* with its conventional court-room style.[76] In
terms of more detailed analysis, there is in *OWS* quite a strong tendency to
avoid hiatus and asyndeton, and this too is not the same in the *Odysseus*;[77]
this actually seems to go against the general tendency for the *Odysseus* to
appear more carefully composed than *OWS*. As for O'Sullivan's strictures on
a tone of 'pervasive sententiousness', this is obviously only intended to apply
to *OWS*,[78] and, whilst Alcidamas does not observe modern Anglo-Saxon

codes of modesty and stakes his claims as a teacher with scant regard for the finer feelings of his rivals, he knows what he is talking about and presents his main thesis with vigour, insight and a commonsense born of experience. He is no great advertisement for elegance, but 'Alcidamas did not look good on papyrus, and he may not look much good to us' is an unworthy epitaph.[79]

The Text

Avezzù's edition is much the most thoroughly researched text available with a description of all the MSS and a fuller *apparatus criticus* than any other edition; he has put all scholars interested in Alcidamas much in his debt. Essentially, nearly all the MSS of Alcidamas' surviving works derive from two: **A**. the Cripps MS (Burney 95 in the British Museum) written in the thirteenth or early fourteenth century AD, which includes the *Odysseus* but not *OWS*, and **X**, the Palatine MS (now in Heidelberg – 88) written in the twelfth century AD, which includes both the *Odysseus* and *OWS*.

I have not always agreed with Avezzù's judgement (whilst gratefully acknowledging his labour), and I have indicated points of disagreement in the Commentary. It would be wrong not to acknowledge also MacDowell's careful examination of the MSS evidence and fine judgement which have added so much to the establishment of the text.

Notes to the Introduction

1. *Suda* i.117; Athenaeus 592c; Dion. Hal. *Isaeus* 19; Elaia's contribution to the Delian Confederacy was only 1000 drachmas per year – see B.D. Meritt, H.T. Wade–Gery, M.F. McGregor, *The Athenian Tribute Lists* (Cambridge,Mass.,1939–53), i.484; iii.200–204; R.Stillwell ed., *The Princeton Encyclopaedia of Classical Sites* (Princeton,1976), 295.

2. *Suda* i.535. It seems perverse to avoid calling Gorgias a sophist, even though his main interests were probably in rhetoric. See E.L. Harrison, 'Was Gorgias a sophist ?', *Phoenix* 18 (1964), 183–92 answering E.R. Dodds ed., *Plato* Gorgias (Oxford,1959), 6–7.

3. See note on *OWS* §34.

4. Aeschines – *Suda* ii.184; [Plut.] *Vitae X Orat.* 840b; Photius, *Bibl.* cod.61, p.20a40 ff. Demosthenes – *Suda* ii.45; Plut. *Demosth.* 5.7; Lucian, *Dem enc. 12.* Kennedy, 237 says there is no evidence that Aeschines studied with any sophist or rhetor, citing the story in one of the anonymous Lives that, when Aeschines was in exile on Rhodes and the Rhodians asked him to teach rhetoric, he disclaimed any knowledge of it. The Lives are, though, inconsistent; another says he set up a school on Rhodes. See M.R. Dilts ed., *Scholia in Aeschinem* (Stuttgart and Leipzig,1992), *Vitae* 1.6; 3.3.

5. *Rhet.* iii.1406a–b. See pp.33–7, 85–7. For the possible influence of Alcidamas on the *Rhetorica ad Alexandrum*, see K. Barwick, 'Die "Rhetorik ad Alexandrum" und Anaximenes, Alkidamas, Isokrates, Aristoteles und die Theodekteia', *Philologus* 110 (1966), 219–22.

6. *Suda* i.535.

7. Diog. Laert. 9.54; *Suda* iv.247; Tzetzes, *Chiliades* 12.571.

8. *Tusc. Disp.* i.48.116.

9. τὸν οὖν Ἐλεατικὸν Παλαμήδην ... Quint. 3.1.8ff. Quintilian's identification of the 'Eleatic Palamedes' with 'Alcidamas Elaites' is rejected by all editors of the *Phaedrus* in favour of Zeno (following the scholiast and Diog. Laert. 9.250), and it is assumed either that Quintilian made a mistake or that the phrase *quem Plato Palameden appellat* is a marginal gloss. Milne, 17–18 and 45 tried to defend the identification with ingenuity but without success. It seems best to take it that Quintilian made a mistake.

10. Tzetzes, *Chiliades* 11.750ff. – caution is probably needed regarding some of Tzetzes' claims – see A.A. Vasiliev, *History of the Byzantine Empire* (Madison, Milwaukee and London,1952), ii.498–9.

11. *Certamen Homeri et Hesiodi* 235 (Allen).

12. H. Rabe ed., *Prolegomenon Sylloge* (Leipzig,1931), 192.

13. See pp.88–9.

14. Diog. Laert. 8.56; See D. O'Brien, 'The relation of Anaxagoras and Empedocles', *JHS* lxxxviii (1968), 94–6.

15. Cic. *Brut.* 46 ff.; Kennedy, 58–61.

16. Cole, 24; for the suggestion that Corax and Tisias may have been the same person, see T. Cole, 'Who was Corax?', *Illinois Classical Studies* 16 (1991), 65–84.

17. Plato, *Hipp. mai.* 282b; Diod. Sic. 12.53.1–2; Thuc. iii.86.3–4.

18. M. Gagarin ed., *Antiphon: The Speeches* (Cambridge,1997), 1–9.

19. Thuc.viii.68. For Antiphon's forensic expertise, see M. Gagarin, *op.cit.*, 16–21.

20. S. Wilcox, 'The scope of early rhetorical instruction', *HSCP* 46 (1942), 121–55.

21. *pace* J.D. Denniston who regarded Gorgias' visit as 'the boundary between the dark ages and the dawn of history' – *Greek Prose Style* (Oxford,1952), 1. For more balanced views, see J. H. Finley Jnr., *Three Essays on Thucydides* (Cambridge, Mass., 1967), 57–88; F. Solmsen, *Intellectual Experiments of the Greek Enlightenment* (Princeton,1975), 24.

22. E.g. Aristoph. *Clouds* 206–8, 494–6; *Birds* 40–41; *Knights* 1316–7; *Wasps passim.*

23. For the difficulties of speaking in the Assembly, see Thuc. iii.38.4. For the competitive atmosphere, see *OWS* §1; Isoc. 13.3, 13.12; 10.1–13; Plato, *Apol.* 20b; *Phaedr.* 269b–c; *Rep.* 600c–d; Xen. *Cyn.* 13; *Rhet ad Alex.* 1421a.

24. See generally M. Lavency, *Aspects de la logographie judiciaire attique* (Louvain,1964), 42, 64ff. On the more positive side the speeches of a successful *logographos* like Lysias were sometimes read for pleasure and edification – S. Usher, 'Lysias and his clients', *GRBS* 17 (1976), 37–9.

25. C. Carey and R.A. Reid eds., *Demosthenes: Selected Private Speeches* (Cambridge,1985), 37–9.

26. *fr.* 140 in V. Rose ed., *Aristotelis Fragmenta* 2nd ed. (Leipzig,1886) = Dion. Hal. *Isoc.* 18.

27. 15.3, 36, 48–50, 227–8, 276; 12.11; 4.11–12.

28. Cole, 80–2, though he is more cautious in 22–4. See also G.A. Kennedy, 'The earliest rhetorical handbooks', *AJP* lxxx (1959), 169–78; M.

Gagarin, 'Probability and persuasion: Plato and early Greek rhetoric' in I. Worthington ed. *Persuasion* (London and New York,1994), 48–9.

29. Aristot. *Soph. Elench.* 183bff.

30. Fragments in V. Rose, *op. cit.* in n. 26, 114–8.

31. H. Blum, *Die antike Mnemotechnik* (Hildesheim,1969), 40–55.

32. N. Loraux trs. A. Sheridan, *The Invention of Athens* (Cambridge,Mass. and London,1986), 56–61.

33. D. Lohmann, *Die Komposition der Reden in der Ilias* (Berlin,1970).

34. Gorgias – Philostr. *Vit.Soph.* 1.9.2; Aelian, *VH* 12.32; Paus. 10.18.7; Pliny, *NH* 33.83. Hippias – Plato, *Hipp. min.* 363c, 368b. Isocrates considered speeches of this type to be performances akin to those of music and poetry – 15.46.

35. *Letter* 1.6.

36. 10.12. See more generally A.S. Pease, 'Things without Honor', *CPh* 21 (1926), 27–42.

37. Isocrates is aware that the elaboration of the display-piece tends to focus attention on the text and the processes of composition – τοὺς μὲν (λόγους) περὶ σπουδαίων πραγμάτων καὶ ἐπειγόντων ῥητορεύεσθαι, τοὺς δὲ πρὸς ἐπίδειξιν καὶ προς ἐργολαβίαν γεγράφθαι. Aristotle too is beginning to describe some aspects of composition in visual terms e.g. the ideal period is εὐσύνοπτον – 'easily encompassed by the eye' – *Rhet.* iii. 1409a.

38. *OWS* §13.

39. The *Suda* says that it was Pericles who was the first to give a written speech in court, and that before him people improvised – iv.100. Cf. Cic. *Brut.* 27.

40. Plato, *Phaedr.* 228. Aristophanes was very familiar with the process and made fun of it – *Knights*, 347–50.

41. Demosthenes once had a lapse of memory before Philip, much to Aeschines' glee – Aeschin.2.34–5. Demosthenes was anxious to avoid the reputation of being too text-bound – he was doubtless sensitive to the criticism of an opponent, Pytheas, who said that his ideas 'smelt of lamp-wick' – Plut. *Dem.* 8.3–4.

42. His celebrated technique of μακρολογία was not just a filibustering device or for exhibition purposes – Aristot. *Rhet.* iii.1418a. For the importance of this technique and its subsequent development, see V.

Buchheit, *Untersuchungen zur Theorie des Genos Epideiktikon von Gorgias bis Aristoteles* (München,1960), 20ff.

43. [Long.] *De sub.* 4.2; Dion. Hal. *Comp. Verb.* 25; Quintil. 10.4.4; [Plut.] *Vit. X Orat.* 837ff.

44. R. Johnson, 'A note on the number of Isocrates' pupils', *AJP* 78 (1957), 297ff.; *id.*, 'Isocrates' methods of teaching', *AJP* 80 (1959), 25ff.

45. J.S. Morrison, 'The origins of Plato's Philosopher–Statesman', *CQ* n.s.8 (1958), 198–218; S. Usher ed., *Isocrates: Greek Orators iii* (Warminster,1990), 7–10.

46. τελεσφόρον τὴν πειθώ – Alcidamas' own phrase with a typically Homeric tinge. See Nos. 8 and 9, p.33.

47. There are some similarities with the claims of medical writers, especially the habit of decrying rivals: see W.H.S. Jones ed. and trans., *Hippocrates* (Loeb – Cambridge, Mass. and London, 1921), i.12–14 (*Ancient Medicine* § 1–2); ii.62–5 (*Regimen in Acute Diseases* § 1–2); ii.140–2 (*The Sacred Disease* § 2); iv.2–5 (*The Nature of Man* §1).

48. Milne, 54–63; N.J. Richardson, 'The Contest of Homer and Hesiod and Alcidamas' *Mouseion*', *CQ* n.s.xxxi (1981), 1–10.

49. L. Spengel, Τεχνῶν Συναγωγή sive *Artium Scriptores* (Stuttgart, 1828), 173–5; J. Vahlen, 'Der Rhetor Alkidamas', *Sitzber. Wien. Akad.* 43 (1863), 491–528; C. Reinhardt, *De aemulis Isocratis* Diss. Bonn, (1873); A. Gercke, 'Isokrates 13 und Alkidamas', *RhM* 54 (1899), 404–13; *id.*,'Die Replik des Isokrates gegen Alkidamas', *RhM* 62 (1907), 170–202; G. Walberer, *Isokrates und Alkidamas,* Diss. Hamburg,1938. O'Sullivan, 24–31 gives a useful and judicious summary of previous discussion. See also Milne, 21–53.

50. For an excellent account of the various stories surrounding Palamedes and their sources, see S. Woodford, 'Palamedes seeks revenge', *JHS* cxiv (1994), 164–9.

51. The idea that Alcidamas may here have remembered and used elements of Eur. *Palamedes*, which was produced with *Alexandros* and *Troades* in 415BC, is intriguing, but has been rejected on good grounds by R. Scodel, *The Trojan Trilogy of Euripides* (Göttingen,1980), 46–7. It is possible that a later episode in the Palamedes tale had some influence on Alcidamas. Oeax, Palamedes' brother, is said to have broadcast the news of Palamedes' death with messages written on oarblades thrown into the sea, one of which reached Nauplios in Euboea. The story is referred to in Aristoph. *Thesm.* 769–75, and explained by the scholiast on l. 771. In view of the fact that Alcidamas does not mention this story in connection with Nauplios, it is possible that the inscriptions on the oarblades suggested the writing on the arrow and the spear.

52. E.g. 'a poor thing' (Guthrie). For the strategy of blackening the opponent's reputation, see Carey and Reid, *op.cit.* in n.41, 9–10.

53. Blass believed that it was a fourth century BC composition, possibly by Polycrates; Brozska did not accept its authenticity and quoted Schöll who placed the speech in the third or perhaps even the second century BC. More recently, Kennedy, 172–3 and Koniaris have again denied its authenticity and O'Sullivan, 90, n.161 seems to agree (it is strange that such a detailed treatment of Alcidamas should only mention the *Odysseus* once in passing). It was defended by Auer who is implicitly accepted by Avezzù, 79, and it was accepted as genuine by Gagarin, though on rather superficial grounds. See F. Blass, *Die attische Beredsamkeit* (Leipzig,1892), ii.359–63; G.L. Koniaris, 'Michigan Papyrus 2754 and the *Certamen*', *HSCP* 75 (1971), 115 n.19; H. Auer, *De Alcidamantis declamatione quae inscribitur* Ὀδυσσεὺς κατὰ Παλαμήδους προδοσίας, Diss. Münster,1913; M. Gagarin, *op. cit.* in n. 40, 67 n.20.

54. See n.9.

55. Strabo 13.3.5; Steph Byz. s.v. Ἐλαία.

56. Coinage – *OWS* §6; *Odysseus* 26. Music – *OWS* §24, 25; *Odysseus* 2.

57. Aristot. *Rhet.* i. 1373b; ii. 1397a.

58. Cic. *Tusc. Disp.* i.48.116. Paradoxical writing on such topics as death or poverty pre-dated rhetorical exercises; Cicero had translated some lines fron Euripides' *Cretans* which reversed conventional ideas about birth and death. The *Encomium of Nais* is attested in Athen. 592c; she evidently had quite a reputation since she is mentioned by Lysias *fr.* 245 (Sauppe) and by Aristophanes in *Gerytades fr.*170 (Kock) and perhaps in *Wealth*, 179 (though the MSS have Λαΐς). The works on Proteus the dog and poverty are attested in Menander Rhetor, *Epid.* iii.346.9–18. The separate existence of the *Encomium of Poverty* was denied by Brzoska on the grounds of a false reading; Russell and Wilson have suggested that the speech should be attributed to Proteus (though no canine nickname is attested for him) – D.A. Russell and N.G. Wilson eds., *Menander Rhetor* (Oxford,1981), *ad loc.* and

249. However, the jokey references in Lucian, *Symp.* 12 to Alcidamas ὁ Κυνικός and his loud bark are very appropriate to someone who has composed a speech about a dog, and I believe that Avezzù is right to accept the text of Menander which identifies two speeches rather than one.

59. Quint. 3.1.8–10; see p.33, No.5; Dion. Hal. *Letter to Ammaios* 1.2 – παραγγελμάτων τεχνικῶν συγγραφεῖς.

60. Diog. Laert. 8.56.

61. F. Nietzsche, 'Der Florentinische Tractat über Homer und Hesiod, ihr Geschlecht und ihren Wettkampf', *RhM* 25 (1870), 528–40; *id.*, *RhM* 28 (1873), 211–49. Nietzsche's views have won much support and now almost amount to orthodoxy. For a very thorough examination of possible connections between Alcidamas and the *Certamen* (granted that Alcidamas wrote an early version of it), see O'Sullivan, 79–105. For a recent sceptical view, see K. Heldmann, *Die Niederlage Homers im Dichterwettstreit mit Hesiod* (Göttingen,1982), 9–14.

62. J.P. Mahaffy ed.,*The Flinders Petrie Papyri* (Dublin,1891), i.70 no.xxv; J.G. Winter, 'A New Fragment on the Life of Homer', *TAPA* 56 (1925), 120–9.

63. F. Solmsen, 'Drei Rekonstruktionen zur antiken Rhetorik und Poetik', *Hermes* 67 (1932), 133–44; R. Pfeiffer, *A History of Classical Scholarship* (Oxford,1968), 51; G.S. Kirk, 'The Michigan Alcidamas–Papyrus; Heraclitus Fr. 56D; the riddle of the lice', *CQ* 44 (1950), 149–67; E.R. Dodds, 'The Alcidamas–Papyrus again', *CQ* n.s.2 (1952), 187–8; M.L. West, ' The contest of Homer and Hesiod', *CQ* n.s.17 (1967), 433–50; N.J. Richardson, *op. cit.* in n.47; W.K.C. Guthrie, *The Sophists* (Cambridge,1971), 313; *OCD³* s.v.Alcidamas.

64. *Contest*, 314 specifically mentions the emperor Hadrian.

65. Stobaeus 4.52.22.

66. *Contest*, 323.

66. Kirk, *op. cit.* in n.61 tried to show that there was a stylistic discrepancy between ll. 1–14 and 15–25 of the papyrus, and this was accepted by Dodds, *op. cit.* n.61. However, although there is an undoubted change – as it were to a concluding paragraph – at that point, a later very rigorous stylistic analysis has made it much harder to maintain a division. See R. Renehan, 'The Michigan Alcidamas–Papyrus: a problem in methodology', *HSCP* 75 (1971), 85–105 esp.103–4; *id., Studies in Greek Texts* (Göttingen,1975), 144–59.

68. *OWS* §2, 29, 31. δι᾽ ἀκριβείας μνήμης is very like Alcidamas.

69. Plato, *Phaedr.* 267c – ...μουσεῖα λόγων – ὡς διπλασιολογίαν καὶ γνωμολογίαν καὶ εἰκονολογίαν ...

70. The fullest modern account of Alcidamas' style is O'Sullivan, 32–42 to which I am much indebted. The acute judgements of Blass are still worth reading – F. Blass, *Die attische Beredsamkeit* (Leipzig,1892), ii.357–9.

71. O'Sullivan, 32–5.

72. S. Usher, review of O'Sullivan in *CQ* 43 (1993), 436.

73. E.g. ἀντίτυπος καὶ προσάντης §6; χρόνου καὶ σχολῆς §8; εἴδωλα καὶ σχήματα καὶ μιμήματα §27.

74. E.g. αὐτοσχεδιασμός §18, 20, 23; εὐπόρημα §26; ὁμοδραμεῖν §7; δυσανάληπτός §19.

75. E.g. *OWS* §4, 20, 25.

76. E.g. *OWS* §8, 15, 20, 28, 34.

77. Blass, *op.cit.* in n. 70, 358.

78. O'Sullivan, 39ff.

79. *ibid.*, 42.

Select Bibliography

Texts and editions

AVEZZU, G, *Alcidamante: orazioni e frammenti* (Rome,1982) – with Italian translation.

BLASS, F., *Antiphontis orationes et fragmenta* (Leipzig,1881).

PAGE, D.L., Additions to the Appendix, *Hesiod, Homeric Hymns, Epic Cycle, Homerica* (Loeb–Cambridge, Mass.,1936), pp.624–7.

RADERMACHER, L., *Artium Scriptores* (Vienna,1951).

WINTER, J.G., 'A New Fragment on the Life of Homer', *TAPA* 56 (1925), 120–9.

Translations (*OWS* only)

MATSON, P., ROLLINSON, R. and SOUSA, M. eds., *Readings from Classical Rhetoric* (Carbondale, Ill.,1990),38–42.

VAN HOOK, L. 'Alcidamas versus Isocrates', *Classical Weekly* 12 (1919), 89–94.

General works

AUER, H., *De Alcidamantis declamatione quae inscribitur* Ὀδυσσεὺς κατὰ Παλαμήδης προδοσίας Diss. Münster,1913.

BARWICK, K., 'Die "Rhetorik ad Alexandrum" und Anaximenes, Alkidamas, Isokrates, Aristoteles und die Theodekteia', *Philologus* 110 (1966), 212–45.

BLASS, F., *Die attische Beredsamkeit* (Leipzig,1892).

BLUM, H., *Die antike Mnemotechnik* (Hildesheim,1969).

BRZOSKA, J., s.v. Alkidamas – *RE* i (1894), 1533–9.

CAREY, C. and REID, R.A.eds., *Demosthenes: Selected Private Speeches* (Cambridge,1985).

CAREY, C. ed., *Lysias: Selected Speeches* (Cambridge,1989).

COLE, T., *The Origins of Rhetoric in Ancient Greece* (Baltimore,1991).

DENNISTON, J.D., *Greek Prose Style* (Oxford,1952).

DODDS, E.R.ed., *Plato,Gorgias* (Oxford,1959).

DODDS, E.R., 'The Alcidamas-Papyrus again', *CQ* n.s.2 (1952), 187–8.

DOVER, K.J., *Greek Popular Morality* (Oxford,1974).

DOVER, K.J., *Lysias and the* Corpus Lysiacum (Berkeley and Los Angeles,1968).

FINLEY,J.H. Jnr., *Three Essays on Thucydides* (Cambridge, Mass.,1967).

GAGARIN, M. ed., *Antiphon:The Speeches* (Cambridge,1997).

GAGARIN, M., 'Probability and persuasion: Plato and early Greek rhetoric' in I. Worthington ed., *Persuasion* (London,1994), 46–68.

GOODY, J and WATT, I., 'The Consequences of Literacy' in J. Goody ed., *Literacy in Traditional Societies* (Cambridge,1968), 27–68.

GUTHRIE, W.K.C., *The Sophists* (Cambridge,1971) = *A History of Greek Philosophy* (Cambridge,1969), iii.part i.

HAVELOCK, E.A.,*The Literate Revolution in Greece and its Cultural Consequences* (Princeton,1982).

HARRIS, W.V., *Ancient Literacy* (Cambridge, Mass. and London,1989).

HELDMANN, K., *Die Niederlage Homers im Dichterwettstreit mit Hesiod* (Göttingen,1982).

HUDSON–WILLIAMS, H.Ll., 'Political speeches in Athens', *CQ* n.s.1 (1951), 68–73.

JEBB, R.C., *The Attic Orators from Antiphon to Isaeus* (London,1876).

KENNEDY, G.A., *The Art of Persuasion in Greece* (Princeton,1963).

KENNEDY, G.A., *A New History of Classical Rhetoric* (Princeton,1994).

KIRK, G.S., 'The Michigan Alcidamas-papyrus; Heraclitus fr.56D; the riddle of the lice', *CQ* n.s.44 (1950), 149–67.

KONIARIS, G.L., 'Michigan Papyrus 2754 and the *Certamen*', *HSCP* 75 (1971), 107–29.

LAVENCY, M., *Aspects de la logographie judiciaire attique* (Louvain,1964).

MACDOWELL, D.M., 'Gorgias, Alcidamas and the Cripps and Palatine Manuscripts', *CQ* n.s.11 (1961), 113–24.

MACDOWELL, D.M. ed., *Gorgias:Encomium of Helen* (Bristol,1982).

MAHAFFY, J.P., *The Flinders Petrie Papyri* vol.i. (Dublin,1891).

MILNE, M.J., *A Study in Alcidamas and his Relation to Contemporary Sophistic*, Diss. Bryn Mawr,1924.

NIETZSCHE, F., 'Die Florentinische Tractat über Homer und Hesiod, ihr Geschlecht und ihren Wettkampf', *RhM* 25 (1870), 528–40; *RhM* 28 (1873), 211.

ONG, W.J., *Orality and Literacy* (London,1982).

O'SULLIVAN, N., *Alcidamas, Aristophanes and the beginnings of Greek stylistic theory* (Stuttgart,1992).

PFEIFFER, R., *History of Classical Scholarship* vol.i (Oxford,1968).

RENEHAN, R., 'The Michigan Alcidamas–Papyrus: A Problem in Methodology', *HSCP* 75 (1971), 85–105.

RENEHAN, R., *Studies in Greek Texts* (Göttingen,1976).

RICHARDSON, N., 'The Contest of Homer and Hesiod and Alcidamas' *Mouseion*', *CQ* n.s. 31 (1981), 1–10.

RUSSELL, D.A., *Criticism in Antiquity* (London,1981).

RUSSELL, D.A., *Greek Declamation* (Cambridge,1983).

SOLMSEN, F., 'Drei Rekonstruktionen zur antiken Rhetorik und Poetik', *Hermes* 67 (1932), 133–44.

STEIDLE, W., 'Redekunst und Bildung bei Isokrates', *Hermes* 80 (1952), 257–96.

THOMAS, R., *Literacy and Orality in Ancient Greece* (Cambridge,1992).

USHER, S.ed., *Greek Orators iii: Isocrates* (Warminster,1990).

USHER, S., *Greek oratory: tradition and originality* (Oxford,1999)

USHER, S., 'Lysias and his clients', *GRBS* 17 (1976), 37–9.

WALBERER, G., *Isokrates und Alkidamas* Diss. Hamburg,1938.

WERSDORFER, H., *Die ΦΙΛΟΣΟΦΙΑ des Isokrates im Spiegel ihrer Terminologie* (Leipzig,1940).

WILCOX, S., 'The scope of early rhetorical instruction', *HSCP* 53 (1942), 121–55.

WORTHINGTON, I. ed., *Persuasion* (London,1994).

Fuller bibliographies can be found in Avezzù and O'Sullivan.

List of abbreviations

Avezzù – Avezzù, G., *Alcidamante; orazioni e frammenti* (Rome, 1982)

Bekker – Bekker, I. ed., *Oratores Attici* (Oxford, 1823 and Berlin, 1824)

Blass – Blass, F., *Antiphontis orationes et fragmenta* (Leipzig, 1881)

Brozska – Broszka, J., *Alkidamas* in *Real-Enzyklopädie der klassischen Altertumswissenschaft* (1894), i.1533–9

Cole – Cole, T., *The Origins of Rhetoric in Ancient Greece* (Baltimore,1991)

DK – Diels, H. and Kranz, W., *Die Fragmente der Vorsokratiker* 5th ed. (Berlin, 1951–2)

Kennedy – Kennedy, G. A., *The Art of Persuasion in Greece* (Princeton, 1963)

Kühner-Gerth[4] – Kühner, R. and Gerth, B., *Ausführliche Grammatik der griechischen Sprache* 4th ed. (Hannover, 1955)

LIMC –*Lexicon Iconographicum Mythologiae Classicae* (Zürich and Munich, 1981-99)

LSJ – Liddell, H.G. and Scott, R. rev. H. Stuart Jones, *Greek-English Lexicon* 9th ed. (Oxford, 1925-40)

MacDowell – MacDowell, D.M., 'Gorgias, Alcidamas and the Cripps and Palatine Manuscripts', *CQ* n.s.11 (1961), 113-4

Milne – Milne, M.J., *A Study in Alcidamas and his Relation to Contemporary Sophistic* Diss., Bryn Mawr, 1924

Odysseus – Alcidamas, *Odysseus: against the treachery of Palamedes*

O'Sullivan – O'Sullivan, N., *Alcidamas, Aristophanes and the beginnings of Greek stylistic theory* (Stuttgart,1992)

OWS – Alcidamas, *On those who write written speeches* or *On sophists*

Radermacher – Radermacher, L.R., *Artium Scriptores* (Vienna,1951)

Reiske – Reiske, I., *Oratorum Graecorum* viii (Leipzig,1773)

Sauppe – Sauppe, H. and Baiter, J.G., *Oratores Attici* viii (Zürich,1848)

Suda – A. Adler ed., *Suidae Lexicon* (Leipzig, 1928-35)

Vahlen – Vahlen, J., *Gesammelte philologische Schriften* (Leipzig and Berlin,1911), i.117-55.

Wersdörfer – Wersdörfer, H., *Die ΦΙΛΟΣΟΦΙΑ des Isokrates im Spiegel ihrer Terminologie* (Leipzig,1940)

ALCIDAMAS
THE WORKS & FRAGMENTS

ΠΕΡΙ ΤΩΝ ΤΟΥΣ ΓΡΑΠΤΟΥΣ ΛΟΓΟΥΣ ΓΡΑΦΟΝΤΩΝ

Η

ΠΕΡΙ ΤΩΝ ΣΟΦΙΣΤΩΝ

(1) ἐπειδή τινες τῶν καλουμένων σοφιστῶν ἱστορίας μὲν καὶ παιδείας ἠμελήκασι καὶ τοῦ δύνασθαι λέγειν ὁμοίως τοῖς ἰδιώταις ἀπείρως ἔχουσι, γράφειν δὲ μεμελετηκότες λόγους καὶ διὰ βιβλίων δεικνύντες τὴν αὑτῶν σοφίαν σεμνύνονται καὶ μέγα φρονοῦσι, καὶ πολλοστὸν μέρος τῆς ῥητορικῆς κεκτημένοι δυνάμεως ὅλης τῆς τέχνης ἀμφισβητοῦσι, διὰ ταύτην τὴν αἰτίαν ἐπιχειρήσω κατηγορίαν ποιήσασθαι τῶν γραπτῶν λόγων, (2) οὐχ ὡς ἀλλοτρίαν ἐμαυτοῦ τὴν δύναμιν αὐτῶν ἡγούμενος, ἀλλ᾽ ὡς ἐφ᾽ ἑτέροις μεῖζον φρονῶν καὶ τὸ γράφειν ἐν παρέργῳ τοῦ < λέγειν > μελετᾶν οἰόμενος χρῆναι, καὶ τοὺς ἐπ᾽ αὐτὸ τοῦτο τὸν βίον καταναλίσκοντας ἀπολελεῖφθαι πολὺ καὶ ῥητορικῆς καὶ φιλοσοφίας ὑπειληφώς, καὶ πολὺ δικαιότερον ἂν ποιητὰς ἢ σοφιστὰς προσαγορεύεσθαι νομίζων. (3) πρῶτον μὲν οὖν ἐντεῦθεν ἄν τις καταφρονήσειε τοῦ γράφειν, ἐξ ὧν ἐστιν εὐεπίθετον καὶ ῥᾴδιον καὶ τῇ τυχούσῃ φύσει πρόχειρον. εἰπεῖν μὲν γὰρ ἐκ τοῦ παραυτίκα περὶ τοῦ παρατυχόντος ἐπιεικῶς, καὶ ταχείᾳ χρήσασθαι τῶν ἐνθυμημάτων καὶ τῶν ὀνομάτων εὐπορίᾳ, καὶ τῷ καιρῷ τῶν πραγμάτων καὶ ταῖς ἐπιθυμίαις τῶν ἀνθρώπων εὐστόχως ἀκολουθῆσαι καὶ τὸν προσήκοντα λόγον εἰπεῖν, οὔτε φύσεως ἁπάσης οὔτε παιδείας τῆς τυχούσης ἐστίν· (4) ἐν πολλῷ δὲ χρόνῳ γράψαι καὶ κατὰ σχολὴν ἐπανορθῶσαι, καὶ παραθέμενον τὰ τῶν προγεγονότων σοφιστῶν συγγράμματα πολλαχόθεν εἰς ταὐτὸν ἐνθυμήματα

On those who write written speeches
or
On sophists

(1) Since some of those who are called sophists have neglected an enquiring approach and training and have no more experience of being able to make speeches than ordinary people, but, having practised the writing of speeches and demonstrating their cleverness through texts, give themselves airs and think much of themselves, and, having acquired a very small part of an orator's ability, lay claim to the art as a whole, this is the reason for my setting out to make a case against written speeches, (2) not because I believe that the ability these people have is foreign to me, but because I pride myself more on other grounds, and think that writing ought to be a by–product of the practice of making speeches, and suppose that those who spend their lives on this particular skill have serious shortcomings in both oratorical skill and in philosophy, and consider that they would much more justly be described as script–writers than as sophists.

(3) First, then, one would look down on writing from this point of view, that it is easy to acquire and simple and readily available to the natural disposition of anyone who happens to want it. For speaking on the spot in a fitting way about whatever presents itself, and employing a swift richness of argument and vocabulary, and following with a sure track the critical moment in affairs and people's inclinations, and using appropriate language is not a universal natural gift nor does it come from just any sort of training. (4) To take a long time over writing, to correct at leisure, to marshal the collected writings of past sophists and bring together ideas from many sources into the same work,

συναγεῖραι καὶ μιμήσασθαι τὰς τῶν εὖ λεγομένων ἐπιτυχίας, καὶ τὰ μὲν ἐκ τῆς τῶν ἰδιωτῶν συμβουλίας ἐπανορθώσασθαι, τὰ δ᾽ αὐτὸν ἐν ἑαυτῷ πολλάκις ἐπισκεψάμενον ἀνακαθῆραι καὶ μεταγράψαι, καὶ τοῖς ἀπαιδεύτοις ῥάδιον πέφυκεν.

(5) ἔστι δ᾽ ἅπαντα τὰ μὲν ἀγαθὰ καὶ καλὰ σπάνια καὶ χαλεπὰ καὶ διὰ πόνων εἰωθότα γίγνεσθαι, τὰ δὲ ταπεινὰ καὶ φαῦλα ῥᾳδίαν ἔχει < τὴν > κτῆσιν· ὥστ᾽ ἐπειδὴ τὸ γράφειν τοῦ λέγειν ἑτοιμότερον ἡμῖν ἐστιν, εἰκότως ἂν αὐτοῦ καὶ τὴν κτῆσιν ἐλάττονος ἀξίας νομίζοιμεν. (6) ἔπειτα τοῖς μὲν λέγειν δεινοῖς οὐδεὶς ἂν φρονῶν ἀπιστήσειεν, ὡς οὐ μικρὸν τὴν τῆς ψυχῆς ἕξιν μεταρρυθμίσαντες ἐπιεικῶς λογογραφήσουσι, τοῖς δὲ γράφειν ἠσκημένοις οὐδεὶς ἂν πιστεύσειεν, ὡς ἀπὸ τῆς αὐτῆς δυνάμεως καὶ λέγειν οἷοί τ᾽ ἔσονται. τοὺς μὲν γὰρ τὰ χαλεπὰ τῶν ἔργων ἐπιτελοῦντας εἰκός, ὅταν ἐπὶ τὰ ῥάω τὴν γνώμην μεταστήσωσιν, εὐπόρως μεταχειρίσασθαι τὴν τῶν πραγμάτων ἀπεργασίαν· τοῖς δὲ τὰ ῥᾴδια γεγυμνασμένοις ἀντίτυπος καὶ προσάντης ἡ τῶν χαλεπωτέρων ἐπιμέλεια καθίσταται. γνοίη δ᾽ ἄν τις ἐκ τῶνδε τῶν παραδειγμάτων· (7) ὁ μὲν γὰρ ἆραι μέγα φορτίον δυνάμενος ἐπὶ τὰ κουφότερα μετελθὼν ῥᾳδίως μεταχειρίσαιτ᾽ ἄν· ὁ δὲ πρὸς τὰ κοῦφα τῇ δυνάμει διικνούμενος οὐδὲν ἂν τῶν βαρυτέρων οἷος τ᾽ εἴη φέρειν. καὶ πάλιν ὁ μὲν ποδώκης δρομεὺς ῥᾳδίως παρέπεσθαι τοῖς βραδυτέροις δύναιτ᾽ ἄν· ὁ δὲ βραδὺς οὐκ ἂν οἷός τ᾽ εἴη τοῖς θάττοσιν ὁμοδραμεῖν. ἔτι δὲ πρὸς τούτοις ὁ μὲν τὰ πόρρω δυνάμενος ἐπισκόπως ἀκοντίζειν ἢ τοξεύειν καὶ τῶν ἐγγὺς τεύξεται ῥᾳδίως· ὁ δὲ τὰ πλησίον βάλλειν ἐπιστάμενος οὔπω δῆλον εἰ καὶ τῶν πόρρω δυνήσεται τυγχάνειν. (8) τὸν αὐτὸν δὴ τρόπον καὶ περὶ τοὺς λόγους ὁ μὲν ἐκ τοῦ παραυτίκα καλῶς αὐτοῖς χρώμενος οὐκ ἄδηλον ὅτι μετὰ χρόνου καὶ σχολῆς ἐν τῷ γράφειν διαφέρων ἔσται λογοποιός· ὁ δ᾽ ἐπὶ τοῦ γράφειν τὰς διατριβὰς

to copy happy expressions in what is well said, to correct some things on the advice of ordinary people and to revise and rewrite others having looked over them by oneself many times, this is naturally easy even for those without training.

(5) Everything good and fine is hard to come by and difficult, and is usually produced by hard work, but what is ordinary and trivial is easy of acquisition. So, since writing is more readily available to us than speaking, it is reasonable that we should consider its acquisition to be of less value too. (6) Then no-one who thinks sensibly would fail to believe that, with a small alteration to their mental framework, those who are good at speaking will write scripts for speeches appropriately, but no-one would believe that those practised in writing will also be able to make a speech as a result of this same ability. It is likely that, whenever people who accomplish difficult tasks turn their minds to easier ones, they will be amply competent to take in hand the completion of them. But, for those who are practised in easier matters, the attention they must devote to more difficult tasks is the reverse of this and is an uphill struggle. One might appreciate this from the following examples : a man able to lift a heavy weight, if he turned to lighter objects, would take them up easily, but someone whose strength went only so far as light objects would not be able to carry any of the heavier ones. And again, the swift runner would easily be able to keep up with slower ones, but the slow runner would not be able to keep pace with the quicker. In addition to this, the man who can hit the target, hurling the javelin or shooting an arrow at things far away, will easily hit those close to as well; but it is by no means clear that the man who knows how to shoot at things close by will also be able to hit those far away. (8) In the same way with regard to speeches too, it is not hard to demonstrate that the man who gives a good account on the spur of the moment will, given time and leisure, be a notable composer of speeches when

ποιούμενος οὐκ ἀφανὲς ὅτι μεταβὰς ἐπὶ τοὺς αὐτοσχεδιαστικοὺς λόγους ἀπορίας καὶ πλάνου καὶ ταραχῆς ἕξει πλήρη τὴν γνώμην.

(9) ἡγοῦμαι δὲ καὶ τῷ βίῳ τῶν ἀνθρώπων τὸ μὲν λέγειν ἀεί τε καὶ διὰ παντὸς χρήσιμον εἶναι, τοῦ δὲ γράφειν ὀλιγάκις εὔκαιρον τὴν δύναμιν αὐτῷ καθίστασθαι. τίς γὰρ οὐκ οἶδεν, ὅτι λέγειν μὲν ἐκ τοῦ παραυτίκα καὶ δημηγοροῦσι καὶ δικαζομένοις καὶ τὰς ἰδίας ὁμιλίας ποιοῦσιν ἀναγκαῖόν ἐστι, καὶ πολλάκις ἀπροσδοκήτως καιροὶ πραγμάτων παραπίπτουσιν, ἐν οἷς οἱ μὲν σιωπῶντες εὐκαταφρόνητοι δόξουσιν εἶναι, τοὺς δὲ λέγοντας ὡς ἰσόθεον τὴν γνώμην ἔχοντας ὑπὸ τῶν ἄλλων τιμωμένους ὁρῶμεν. (10) ὅταν γὰρ νουθετῆσαι δέῃ τοὺς ἁμαρτάνοντας ἢ παραμυθήσασθαι τοὺς δυστυχοῦντας ἢ πραῦναι τοὺς θυμουμένους ἢ τὰς ἐξαίφνης ἐπενεχθείσας αἰτίας ἀπολύσασθαι, τηνικαῦθ᾽ ἡ τοῦ λέγειν δύναμις τῇ χρείᾳ τῶν ἀνθρώπων ἐπικουρεῖν οἷά τ᾽ ἐστίν· ἡ δὲ γραφὴ σχολῆς δεῖται καὶ μακροτέρους ποιεῖται τοὺς χρόνους τῶν καιρῶν· οἱ μὲν γὰρ ταχεῖαν τὴν ἐπικουρίαν ἐπὶ τῶν ἀγώνων ἀπαιτοῦσιν, ἡ δὲ κατὰ σχολὴν καὶ βραδέως ἐπιτελεῖ τοὺς λόγους. ὥστε τίς ἂν φρονῶν ταύτην τὴν δύναμιν ζηλώσειεν, ἢ τῶν καιρῶν τοσοῦτον ἀπολείπεται;

(11) πῶς δ᾽ οὐ καταγέλαστον, εἰ τοῦ κήρυκος παρακαλοῦντος "τίς ἀγορεύειν βούλεται τῶν πολιτῶν;" ἢ τοῦ ὕδατος ἐν τοῖς δικαστηρίοις ἤδη ῥέοντος, ἐπὶ τὸ γραμματεῖον ὁ ῥήτωρ πορεύοιτο συνθήσων καὶ μαθησόμενος λόγον; ὡς ἀληθῶς γὰρ εἰ μὲν ἦμεν τύραννοι τῶν πόλεων, ἐφ᾽ ἡμῖν ἂν ἦν καὶ δικαστήρια συλλέγειν καὶ περὶ τῶν κοινῶν βουλεύεσθαι πραγμάτων, ὥσθ᾽, ὁπότε γράψαιμεν τοὺς λόγους, τηνικαῦτα τοὺς ἄλλους πολίτας ἐπὶ τὴν ἀκρόασιν παρακαλεῖν. ἐπεὶ δ᾽ ἕτεροι τούτων κύριοί εἰσιν, ἆρ᾽ οὐκ

it comes to writing; but it is not hard to see that, if one who spends his time writing changes over to extempore speeches, he will have a mind full of helplessness, wandering and confusion.

(9) I think that in the life of men also making speeches is both constantly and in every circumstance useful, but writing ability is seldom apt for the critical moment. For who does not know that making speeches on the spot is necessary both for those who address the people and for those who go to court and for those who take part in private gatherings, and opportunities often occur unexpectedly in circumstances where those who stay silent will seem justly reviled while we see those who can speak honoured by others as if they had a god-like intellect. (10) For, whenever it is necessary to admonish those who are going astray or to counsel the unfortunate or to calm those moved by passion or to rebut accusations brought out of the blue, then the ability to make a speech can be a help in people's hour of need. But writing needs leisure and requires more time than opportunities allow. For people ask for speedy help in their law-suits whilst writing produces speeches at leisure and slowly. So, what sensible person would envy this ability which falls so far short of the opportunities ? (11) Would it not be ridiculous if, when the herald was proclaiming 'Which of the citizens wishes to speak ?', or when the water-clock in the courts was already running, the speaker were to proceed to his writing tablet in order to assemble and con his speech ? For, if we were tyrants in charge of cities, it would truly be in our power both to summon the courts and to take counsel for public affairs so that, whenever we wrote speeches, we could then call the other citizens to listen to them. But since it is others who are in control of these things, is it not silly of us to

εὔηθες ἡμᾶς ἄλλην τινὰ ποιεῖσθαι μελέτην λόγων † ἐναντίως
ἔχουσιν ἀκριβῶς † < .... > (12) εἰ γὰρ οἱ τοῖς ὀνόμασιν
ἐξειργασμένοι καὶ μᾶλλον ποιήμασιν ἢ λόγοις ἐοικότες καὶ
τὸ μὲν αὐτόματον καὶ πλέον ἀληθείαις ὅμοιον
ἀποβεβληκότες, μετὰ παρασκευῆς δὲ πεπλάσθαι καὶ
συγκεῖσθαι δοκοῦντες, ἀπιστίας καὶ φθόνου τὰς τῶν
ἀκουόντων γνώμας ἐμπιμπλᾶσι < .... > (13) τεκμήριον δὲ
μέγιστον· οἱ γὰρ εἰς τὰ δικαστήρια τοὺς λόγους γράφοντες
φεύγουσι τὰς ἀκριβείας καὶ μιμοῦνται τὰς τῶν
αὐτοσχεδιαζόντων ἑρμηνείας, καὶ τότε κάλλιστα γράφειν
δοκοῦσιν, ὅταν ἥκιστα γεγραμμένοις ὁμοίους πορίσωνται
λόγους. ὁπότε δὲ καὶ τοῖς λογογράφοις τοῦτο πέρας τῆς
ἐπιεικείας ἐστίν, ὅταν τοὺς αὐτοσχεδιάζοντας μιμήσωνται,
πῶς οὐ χρὴ καὶ τῆς παιδείας ἐκεῖνο μάλιστα τιμᾶν, ἀφ' οὗ
πρὸς τοῦτο τὸ γένος τῶν λόγων εὐπόρως ἕξομεν;

(14) οἶμαι δὲ καὶ διὰ τοῦτ' ἄξιον εἶναι τοὺς γραπτοὺς
λόγους ἀποδοκιμάζειν, ὅτι τὸν βίον τῶν μεταχειριζομένων
ἀνώμαλον καθιστᾶσι. περὶ πάντων μὲν γὰρ τῶν πραγμάτων
γεγραμμένους ἐπίστασθαι λόγους ἕν τι τῶν ἀδυνάτων πέφυκεν·
ἀνάγκη δ' ἐστίν, ὅταν τις τὰ μὲν αὐτοσχεδιάζῃ, τὰ δὲ τυποῖ,
τὸν λόγον ἀνόμοιον ὄντα ψόγον τῷ λέγοντι παρασκευάζειν,
καὶ τὰ μὲν ὑποκρίσει καὶ ῥαψῳδίᾳ παραπλήσια δοκεῖν
εἶναι, τὰ δὲ ταπεινὰ καὶ φαῦλα φαίνεσθαι παρὰ τὴν ἐκείνων
ἀκρίβειαν. (15) δεινὸν δ' ἐστὶ τὸν ἀντιποιούμενον φιλοσοφίας
{ἀντιλέγειν} καὶ παιδεύσειν ἑτέρους ὑπισχνούμενον, ἂν μὲν
ἔχῃ γραμματεῖον ἢ βιβλίον, δεικνύναι δύνασθαι τὴν αὑτοῦ
σοφίαν, ἂν δὲ τούτων ἄμοιρος γένηται, μηδὲν τῶν ἀπαιδεύτων
βελτίω καθεστάναι, καὶ χρόνου μὲν δοθέντος δύνασθαι
λόγον ἐξενεγκεῖν, εὐθέως δὲ περὶ τοῦ προτεθέντος ἀφωνότερον
εἶναι τῶν ἰδιωτῶν, καὶ λόγων μὲν τέχνας ἐπαγγέλλεσθαι, τοῦ
δὲ λέγειν μηδὲ μικρὰν δύναμιν ἔχοντ' ἐν ἑαυτῷ φαίνεσθαι.

adopt another practice with regard to speeches † for those clearly in the contrary position † < .... >. (12) For if speeches which have their text carefully worked out and are more like scripts than speeches and have abandoned both the spontaneous and that which more closely resembles the truth and seem to be moulded by and consist in pre-fabrication fill the minds of their hearers with distrust and resentment < .... > (13) And the following is a most powerful proof: those who write speeches for the courts avoid precision and mimic the style of extempore speakers, and they seem to be doing their best writing when they produce speeches which least resemble scripts. And since this is the touchstone of plausibility even for speech-writers, is it not right to respect most that type of training by which we shall be amply equipped for making speeches of this kind ?

(14) And I think that for this too it is right to make written speeches fail the test for they make life uneven for those who undertake them. For having written speeches in the mind about everything is naturally one of life's impossibilities. And it is inevitable that, whenever someone speaks extempore on some matters and on others hammers out a text, his speech with differences of style will produce criticism for the speaker, the text seeming more suited to the stage or a recital, with the extempore speech seeming common and trivial beside the precise style of the text. (15) And it is a terrible thing if the man who lays claim to philosophy, promising to educate others, can demonstrate his wisdom if he has his writing tablet or his book, but, if he is separated from them, is in no better state than the uneducated, and can produce a speech when given time, but on the spur of the moment is more lost for words about something set before him than the man-in-the-street, and professes technical skill in oratory but clearly has in him not even a small

καὶ γὰρ ἡ μελέτη τοῦ γράφειν ἀπορίαν τοῦ λέγειν πλείστην παραδίδωσιν.

(16) ὅταν γάρ τις ἐθισθῇ κατὰ μικρὸν ἐξεργάζεσθαι τοὺς λόγους καὶ μετ᾽ ἀκριβείας καὶ ῥυθμοῦ τὰ ῥήματα συντιθέναι, καὶ βραδείᾳ τῇ τῆς διανοίας κινήσει χρώμενος ἐπιτελεῖν τὴν ἑρμηνείαν, ἀναγκαῖόν ἐστι τοῦτον, ὅταν εἰς τοὺς αὐτοσχεδιαστοὺς ἔλθῃ λόγους, ἐναντία πράττοντα ταῖς συνηθείαις ἀπορίας καὶ θορύβου πλήρη τὴν γνώμην ἔχειν, καὶ πρὸς ἅπαντα μὲν δυσχεραίνειν, μηδὲν δὲ διαφέρειν τῶν ἰσχνοφώνων, οὐδέποτε δ᾽ εὐλύτῳ τῇ τῆς ψυχῆς ἀγχινοίᾳ χρώμενον ὑγρῶς καὶ φιλανθρώπως μεταχειρίζεσθαι τοὺς λόγους. (17) ἀλλ᾽ ὥσπερ οἱ διὰ μακρῶν χρόνων ἐκ δεσμῶν λυθέντες οὐ δύνανται τοῖς ἄλλοις ὁμοίαν ποιήσασθαι τὴν ὁδοιπορίαν, ἀλλ᾽ εἰς ἐκεῖνα τὰ σχήματα καὶ τοὺς ῥυθμοὺς ἀποφέρονται, μεθ᾽ ὧν καὶ δεδεμένοις αὐτοῖς ἀναγκαῖον ἦν πορεύεσθαι, τὸν αὐτὸν τρόπον ἡ γραφὴ βραδείας τὰς διαβάσεις τῇ γνώμῃ παρασκευάζουσα καὶ τοῦ λέγειν ἐν τοῖς ἐναντίοις ἔθεσι ποιουμένη τὴν ἄσκησιν ἄπορον καὶ δεσμῶτιν τὴν ψυχὴν καθίστησι καὶ τῆς ἐν τοῖς αὐτοσχεδιαστοῖς εὐροίας ἁπάσης ἐπίπροσθεν γίγνεται.

(18) νομίζω δὲ καὶ τὴν μάθησιν τῶν γραπτῶν λόγων χαλεπὴν καὶ τὴν μνήμην ἐπίπονον καὶ τὴν λήθην αἰσχρὰν ἐν τοῖς ἀγῶσι γίγνεσθαι. πάντες γὰρ ἂν ὁμολογήσειαν τὰ μικρὰ τῶν μεγάλων καὶ τὰ πολλὰ τῶν ὀλίγων χαλεπώτερον εἶναι μαθεῖν καὶ μνημονεῦσαι. περὶ μὲν οὖν τοὺς αὐτοσχεδιασμοὺς ἐπὶ τῶν ἐνθυμημάτων δεῖ μόνον τὴν γνώμην ἔχειν, τοῖς δ᾽ ὀνόμασιν ἐκ τοῦ παραυτίκα δηλοῦν· ἐν δὲ τοῖς γραπτοῖς λόγοις καὶ τῶν ἐνθυμημάτων καὶ τῶν ὀνομάτων καὶ < τῶν > συλλαβῶν ἀναγκαῖόν ἐστι ποιεῖσθαι τὴν μνήμην καὶ τὴν μάθησιν ἀκριβῆ. (19) ἐνθυμήματα μὲν οὖν ὀλίγα καὶ μεγάλα

capacity for making a speech. For practising writing results in very great helplessness when it comes to speaking.

(16) For whenever someone has been accustomed to work out speeches in detail and to construct sentences paying attention to both precise wording and rhythm and puts over his interpretation making use of a slow mental process, it is inevitable that, whenever this man comes to extempore speeches, doing the opposite of what he is used to, he should have a mind full of helplessness and panic and should be ill-at-ease with everything, in no way different from those with speech impediments, never using a free readiness of wit to execute his speeches with flexibility and in a way that people like. (17) But, just as those who have been released from their chains after a long period cannot adopt a mode of walking like other people but keep being drawn back to those actions and patterns of movement with which they had to walk when they were tied up, so, in the same way, writing, rendering processes in the mind slow and exercising the practice of speaking in an opposite set of habits, puts the soul too in a state of perplexity and bondage and gets in the way of all that easy flow to be found in extempore speeches.

(18) And I think that both learning written speeches is hard, and holding them in the memory troublesome, and forgetting them in court-cases embarrassing. For everyone would agree that it is harder to learn and remember small matters rather than great and many things rather than few. With regard to extempore speeches then, one only has to pay attention to the arguments and to express them in words as the moment demands. But in written speeches it is necessary to commit to memory and learn precisely both the arguments and the words and the syllables. (19) Further, the arguments in speeches are few

τοῖς λόγοις ἔνεστιν, ὀνόματα δὲ καὶ ῥήματα πολλὰ καὶ ταπεινὰ καὶ μικρὸν ἀλλήλων διαφέροντα, καὶ τῶν μὲν ἐνθυμημάτων ἅπαξ ἕκαστον δηλοῦται, τοῖς δ' ὀνόμασι πολλάκις τοῖς αὐτοῖς ἀναγκαζόμεθα χρῆσθαι· διὸ τῶν μὲν εὔπορος ἡ μνήμη, τοῖς δὲ δυσανάληπτος ἡ μνήμη καὶ δυσφύλακτος ἡ μάθησις καθέστηκεν. (20) ἔτι τοίνυν αἱ λῆθαι περὶ μὲν τοὺς αὐτοσχεδιασμοὺς ἄδηλον τὴν αἰσχύνην ἔχουσιν. εὐλύτου γὰρ τῆς ἑρμηνείας οὔσης καὶ τῶν ὀνομάτων οὐκ ἀκριβῶς συνεξεσμένων, ἂν ἄρα καὶ διαφύγῃ τι τῶν ἐνθυμημάτων, οὐ χαλεπὸν ὑπερβῆναι τῷ ῥήτορι καὶ τῶν ἐφεξῆς ἐνθυμημάτων ἁψάμενον μηδεμιᾷ τὸν λόγον αἰσχύνῃ περιβαλεῖν, ἀλλὰ καὶ τῶν διαφυγόντων, ἂν ὕστερον ἀναμνησθῇ, ῥᾴδιον ποιήσασθαι τὴν δήλωσιν. (21) τοῖς δὲ γεγραμμένα λέγουσιν, ἂν καὶ μικρὸν ὑπὸ τῆς ἀγωνίας ἐκλίπωσί τι καὶ παραλλάξωσιν, ἀπορίαν ἀνάγκη καὶ πλάνον καὶ ζήτησιν ἐγγενέσθαι, καὶ μακροὺς μὲν χρόνους ἐπίσχειν, πολλάκις δὲ τῇ σιωπῇ διαλαμβάνειν τὸν λόγον, ἀσχήμονα δὲ καὶ καταγέλαστον καὶ δυσεπικούρητον καθεστάναι τὴν ἀπορίαν.

(22) ἡγοῦμαι δὲ καὶ ταῖς ἐπιθυμίαις τῶν ἀκροατῶν ἄμεινον χρῆσθαι τοὺς αὐτοσχεδιάζοντας τῶν τὰ γεγραμμένα λεγόντων. οἱ μὲν γὰρ πολὺ πρὸ τῶν ἀγώνων τὰ συγγράμματα διαπονήσαντες ἐνίοτε τῶν καιρῶν ἁμαρτάνουσιν· ἢ γὰρ μακρότερα τῆς ἐπιθυμίας λέγοντες ἀπεχθάνονται τοῖς ἀκούουσιν ἢ βουλομένων ἔτι τῶν ἀνθρώπων ἀκροᾶσθαι προαπολείπουσι λόγους. (23) χαλεπὸν γάρ, ἴσως δ' ἀδύνατόν ἐστιν ἀνθρωπίνην πρόνοιαν ἐφικέσθαι τοῦ μέλλοντος, ὥστε προϊδεῖν ἀκριβῶς, τίνα τρόπον αἱ γνῶμαι τῶν ἀκουόντων πρὸς τὰ μήκη τῶν λεγομένων ἕξουσιν. ἐν δὲ τοῖς αὐτοσχεδιασμοῖς ἐπὶ τῷ λέγοντι γίγνεται ταμιεύεσθαι τοὺς λόγους πρὸς τὰς δυνάμεις τῶν γνωμῶν ἀποβλέποντι, καὶ τὰ

and important, but there are many common words and expressions differing little from each other, and each of the arguments is produced once whilst we are compelled to use the same words on many occasions. Because of this, memory has a good capacity for the former, but, for the latter, memory is hard to acquire and comprehension hard to preserve. (20) So then, lapses of memory in extempore speeches keep their embarrassment hidden. For, since the style is flexible and the words are not polished with great care, if any of the arguments escape the mind, it is not hard for the speaker to pass over them and, taking the arguments which come after, not to incur any embarrassment over his speech, and it is also the case that, if he remembers them afterwards, it is easy to deploy those which escaped him. (21) But, if those speaking to a written text omit or alter even a small thing through stress, they necessarily find themselves in the midst of helplessness, wandering and searching for words ; they pause for long periods, they often break off their speech in silence, and their helplessness appears unseemly, ridiculous and hard to remedy.

(22) And I think that extempore speakers make better use of the inclinations of their audience than those speaking to a written text. For those who take much trouble over their scripts in advance of law-suits sometimes miss the critical opportunities; for they either speak at greater length than people wish and are disliked by their audience, or, when people want to go on listening, they leave off speaking too soon. (23) For it is hard, perhaps impossible, for the human mind to forecast the future in such a way as to foresee precisely what the attitudes of listeners will be with regard to the length of what is being said. But in extempore speeches it is in the power of the speaker to husband arguments, paying attention to the effects of words, both shortening

μήκη συντέμνειν καὶ τὰ συντόμως ἐσκεμμένα διὰ μακροτέρων δηλοῦν.

(24) χωρὶς τοίνυν τούτων οὐδὲ τοῖς παρ᾽ αὐτῶν τῶν ἀγώνων ἐνθυμήμασι διδομένοις ὁμοίως ὁρῶμεν ἑκατέρους χρῆσθαι δυναμένους. τοῖς μὲν γὰρ ἄγραφα λέγουσιν, ἄν τι παρὰ τῶν ἀντιδίκων ἐνθύμημα λάβωσιν ἢ διὰ τὴν συντονίαν τῆς διανοίας αὐτῶν παρὰ σφῶν αὐτῶν διανοηθῶσιν, εὔπορόν ἐστιν ἐν τάξει θεῖναι· τοῖς γὰρ ὀνόμασιν ἐκ τοῦ παραυτίκα περὶ ἁπάντων δηλοῦντες, οὐδ᾽ ὅταν πλείω τῶν ἐσκεμμένων λέγωσιν, οὐδαμῇ τὸν λόγον ἀνώμαλον καὶ ταραχώδη καθιστᾶσι. (25) τοῖς δὲ μετὰ τῶν γραπτῶν λόγων ἀγωνιζομένοις, ἂν ἄρα τι χωρὶς τῆς παρασκευῆς ἐνθύμημα δοθῇ, χαλεπὸν ἐναρμόσαι καὶ χρῆσθαι κατὰ τρόπον· αἱ γὰρ ἀκρίβειαι τῆς τῶν ὀνομάτων ἐξεργασίας οὐ παραδέχονται τοὺς αὐτοματισμούς, ἀλλ᾽ ἀναγκαῖον ἢ μηδὲν χρῆσθαι τοῖς ἀπὸ τῆς τύχης ἐνθυμήμασι δοθεῖσιν, ἢ χρώμενον διαλύειν καὶ συνερείπειν τὴν τῶν ὀνομάτων οἰκονομίαν, καὶ τὰ μὲν ἀκριβῶς τὰ δ᾽ εἰκῇ λέγοντα ταραχώδη καὶ διάφωνον καθιστάναι τὴν ἑρμηνείαν. (26) καίτοι τίς ἂν εὖ φρονῶν ἀποδέξαιτο τὴν τοιαύτην μελέτην, ἥτις καὶ τῶν αὐτομάτων ἀγαθῶν ἐπίπροσθεν τῇ χρήσει καθέστηκε καὶ χείρω τῆς τύχης ἐνίοτε τοῖς ἀγωνιζομένοις τὴν ἐπικουρίαν παραδίδωσι, καὶ τῶν ἄλλων τεχνῶν ἐπὶ τὸ βέλτιον ἄγειν τὸν τῶν ἀνθρώπων βίον εἰθισμένων αὕτη καὶ τοῖς αὐτομάτοις εὐπορήμασιν ἐμποδών ἐστιν;

(27) ἡγοῦμαι δ᾽ οὐδὲ λόγους δίκαιον εἶναι καλεῖσθαι τοὺς γεγραμμένους, ἀλλ᾽ ὥσπερ εἴδωλα καὶ σχήματα καὶ μιμήματα λόγων, καὶ τὴν αὐτὴν κατ᾽ αὐτῶν εἰκότως ἂν δόξαν ἔχοιμεν, ἥπερ καὶ κατὰ τῶν χαλκῶν ἀνδριάντων καὶ λιθίνων ἀγαλμάτων καὶ γεγραμμένων ζῴων. ὥσπερ γὰρ ταῦτα

what is lengthy and setting out what is concisely conceived on a broader scale. (24) Further and apart from this, we can see that these two sets of people cannot make the same kind of use even of arguments which are presented to them in actual law-suits. For those speaking without a text are easily capable of fitting in to their structure any argument they may take from their opponents or any idea they conceive of their own accord since their intellect is at full stretch. For, because they are setting everything out on the spur of the moment, they produce a speech which is by no means uneven and confused, even when they say more than they planned. (25) But for those fighting law-suits with written speeches, if some argument is presented beyond what has been prepared, it is hard to fit it in and use it in the proper way; for the precision of working out the words in the text does not admit of improvisation, but it is necessary either to make no use of arguments presented by chance or, if one does use them, to undo and unbalance the disposition of the text, so that saying some things with precision and others at random renders the style confused and discordant. (26) Now, who in his right mind would adopt such a practice which sets itself against the use of even those advantages which come of their own accord, and which sometimes give parties to a suit less help than chance would offer, and, while other arts customarily lead human life towards improvement, this one gets in the way of even gratuitous resource ?

(27) And I do not think it is right that speeches written down should even be called speeches, but should be thought of as images and patterns and imitations of speeches, and we could reasonably have the same opinion about them as we have about bronze statues and stone monuments and depictions of

μιμήματα τῶν ἀληθινῶν σωμάτων ἐστί, καὶ τέρψιν μὲν ἐπὶ
τῆς θεωρίας ἔχει, χρῆσιν δ' οὐδεμίαν τῷ τῶν ἀνθρώπων βίῳ
παραδίδωσι, (28) τὸν αὐτὸν τρόπον ὁ γεγραμμένος λόγος, ἑνὶ
σχήματι καὶ τάξει κεχρημένος, ἐκ βιβλίου < μὲν >
θεωρούμενος ἔχει τινὰς ἐκπλήξεις, ἐπὶ δὲ τῶν καιρῶν
ἀκίνητος ὢν οὐδεμίαν ὠφέλειαν τοῖς κεκτημένοις
παραδίδωσιν. ἀλλ' ὥσπερ ἀνδριάντων καλῶν ἀληθινὰ
σώματα πολὺ χείρους τὰς εὐμορφίας ἔχοντα πολλαπλασίους
ἐπὶ τῶν ἔργων τὰς ὠφελείας παραδίδωσιν, οὕτω καὶ λόγος ὁ
μὲν ἀπ' αὐτῆς τῆς διανοίας ἐν τῷ παραυτίκα λεγόμενος
ἔμψυχός ἐστι καὶ ζῇ καὶ τοῖς πράγμασιν ἕπεται καὶ τοῖς
ἀληθέσιν ἀφωμοίωται σώμασιν, ὁ δὲ γεγραμμένος εἰκόνι
λόγου τὴν φύσιν ὁμοίαν ἔχων ἁπάσης ἐνεργείας ἄμοιρος
καθέστηκεν.

(29) ἴσως ἂν εἴποι τις ὡς ἄλογόν ἐστι κατηγορεῖν μὲν τῆς
γραφικῆς δυνάμεως, αὐτὸν δὲ διὰ ταύτης φαίνεσθαι τὰς
ἀποδείξεις ποιούμενον, καὶ προδιαβάλλειν τὴν πραγματείαν
ταύτην δι' ἧς εὐδοκιμεῖν παρασκευάζεται παρὰ τοῖς
Ἕλλησιν, ἔτι δὲ περὶ φιλοσοφίαν διατρίβοντα τοὺς
αὐτοσχεδιαστικοὺς λόγους ἐπαινεῖν, καὶ προυργιαίτερον
ἡγεῖσθαι τὴν τύχην τῆς προνοίας καὶ φρονιμωτέρους τοὺς
εἰκῇ λέγοντας τῶν μετὰ παρασκευῆς γραφόντων. (30) ἐγὼ δὲ
πρῶτον μὲν οὐ παντελῶς ἀποδοκιμάζων τὴν γραφικὴν
δύναμιν, ἀλλὰ χείρω τῆς αὐτοσχεδιαστικῆς ἡγούμενος εἶναι,
καὶ τοῦ δύνασθαι λέγειν πλείστην ἐπιμέλειαν οἰόμενος
χρῆναι ποιεῖσθαι, τούτους εἴρηκα τοὺς λόγους· ἔπειτα προσ-
χρῶμαι τῷ γράφειν οὐκ ἐπὶ τούτῳ μέγιστον φρονῶν, ἀλλ' ἵν'
ἐπιδείξω τοῖς ἐπὶ ταύτῃ τῇ δυνάμει σεμνυνομένοις, ὅτι μικρὰ
πονήσαντες ἡμεῖς ἀποκρύψαι καὶ καταλῦσαι τοὺς λόγους
αὐτῶν οἷοί τ' ἐσόμεθα.

animals. For, just as these are imitations of real bodies and give delight to the view but offer no use in human life, (28) in the same way the written speech, having a single form and arrangement, produces certain striking effects when it is conned from the book, but, being fixedly unable to respond to critical moments, is of no use to those who have got hold of it. Just as real bodies present an appearance far inferior to that of fine statues but yet are many times more useful for getting things done, so too the speech spoken straight from the heart on the spur of the moment has a soul in it and is alive and follows upon events and is like those real bodies, while the written speech whose nature corresponds to a representation of the real thing lacks any kind of living power.

(29) Perhaps someone would say that it is illogical to bring accusations against the ability to write whilst oneself being seen to produce public demonstrations in this medium, and to criticise the activity by means of which one tries to get a reputation among the Greeks, and, while spending one's time on methodical study, to praise extempore speeches, and to consider chance more serviceable for the task than forethought and those who improvise more prudent than those who write after preparation. (30) But I have said these words, first of all, not because I wish to dismiss entirely the ability to write but because I consider it inferior to the ability of performing extempore, and believe that one ought to devote the greatest care to the ability to make speeches; second, I am making use of writing with no claims to being outstanding on this account but so that I may demonstrate to those who are boastful because they have this ability that we, with only a little effort, will be able to blot out and destroy their arguments. (31) In addition, I

(31) πρὸς δὲ τούτοις καὶ τῶν ἐπιδείξεων εἵνεκα τῶν εἰς τοὺς ὄχλους ἐκφερομένων ἅπτομαι τοῦ γράφειν. τοῖς μὲν γὰρ πολλάκις ἡμῖν ἐντυγχάνουσιν ἐξ ἐκείνου τοῦ τρόπου παρακελευόμεθα πεῖραν ἡμῶν λαμβάνειν, ὅταν ὑπὲρ ἅπαντος τοῦ προτεθέντος εὐκαίρως καὶ μουσικῶς εἰπεῖν οἷοί τ᾽ ὦμεν· τοῖς δὲ διὰ χρόνου μὲν ἐπὶ τὰς ἀκροάσεις ἀφιγμένοις, μηδεπώποτε δὲ πρότερον ἡμῖν ἐντετυχηκόσιν, ἐπιχειροῦμέν τι δεικνύναι τῶν γεγραμμένων· εἰθισμένοι γὰρ ἀκροᾶσθαι τῶν ἄλλων <τοὺς γραπτ>οὺς λόγους, ἴσως ἂν ἡμῶν αὐτοσχεδιαζόντων ἀκούοντες ἐλάττονα τῆς ἀξίας δόξαν καθ᾽ ἡμῶν λάβοιεν. (32) χωρὶς δὲ τούτων καὶ σημεῖα τῆς ἐπιδόσεως, ἣν εἰκὸς ἐν τῇ διανοίᾳ γίγνεσθαι, παρὰ τῶν γραπτῶν λόγων ἐναργέστατα κατιδεῖν ἔστιν. εἰ μὲν γὰρ βέλτιον αὐτοσχεδιάζομεν νῦν ἢ πρότερον, οὐ ῥᾴδιον ἐπικρίνειν ἐστί, χαλεπαὶ γὰρ αἱ μνῆμαι τῶν προειρημένων λόγων καθεστήκασιν· εἰς δὲ τὰ γεγραμμένα κατιδόντας ὥσπερ ἐν κατόπτρῳ θεωρῆσαι τὰς τῆς ψυχῆς ἐπιδόσεις ῥᾴδιόν ἐστιν. ἔτι δὲ καὶ μνημεῖα καταλιπεῖν ἡμῶν αὐτῶν σπουδάζοντες καὶ τῇ φιλοτιμίᾳ χαριζόμενοι λόγους γράφειν ἐπιχειροῦμεν.

(33) ἀλλὰ μὴν οὐδ᾽ ὡς εἰκῇ λέγειν παρακελευόμεθα, τὴν αὐτοσχεδιαστικὴν δύναμιν τῆς γραφικῆς προτιμῶντες, ἄξιόν ἐστι πιστεύειν. τοῖς μὲν γὰρ ἐνθυμήμασι καὶ τῇ τάξει μετὰ προνοίας ἡγούμεθα δεῖν χρῆσθαι τοὺς ῥήτορας, περὶ δὲ τὴν τῶν ὀνομάτων δήλωσιν αὐτοσχεδιάζειν. οὐ γὰρ τοσαύτην ὠφέλειαν αἱ τῶν γραπτῶν λόγων ἀκρίβειαι παραδιδόασιν, ὅσην εὐκαιρίαν αἱ τῶν ἐκ τοῦ παραχρῆμα λεγομένων δηλώσεις ἔχουσιν. (34) ὅστις οὖν ἐπιθυμεῖ ῥήτωρ γενέσθαι δεινὸς ἀλλὰ μὴ ποιητὴς λόγων ἱκανός, καὶ βούλεται μᾶλλον τοῖς καιροῖς χρῆσθαι καλῶς ἢ τοῖς ὀνόμασι λέγειν ἀκριβῶς, καὶ τὴν εὔνοιαν τῶν ἀκρωμένων ἐπίκουρον ἔχειν σπουδάζει

employ writing for the popular dissemination of my display-performances too. For, whenever we are able to speak on any subject put before us with happy appropriateness for the occasion and with elegance, it is in this mode that we recommend those who meet us often to sample our ability ; but for those who come to hear us after some time and for those who have never before met us, we try to show something of what we have done in writing. For those who have been accustomed to listen to the written speeches of others would perhaps, if they hear us speaking extempore, form a lower opinion of us than we deserve. (32) And, apart from this, signs of progress which are likely to be produced in the mind are very clear to see in the context of written speeches. It is, though, not easy to judge if our extempore speaking is better than it was before, for the recollection of what has been said is difficult. But it is easy by examining written texts to contemplate, as it were in a mirror, the progress of the soul. Also, we undertake the writing of speeches both because we are eager to leave behind memorials of ourselves and to gratify our ambition.

(33) All the same one must not even so believe that, in recommending improvisation, we are giving the ability to speak extempore pride of place over the ability to write. For we consider that speakers must take thought in advance in the use of arguments and structure, but concerning the expression in words they must improvise. For the benefits of the precise style of written speeches are outweighed by the appropriateness to the occasion of expressing things spoken on the spur of the moment. (34) Therefore the man who wishes to be not just an adequate script-writer but a skilled orator, who wants to make good use of the critical moments rather than be meticulous about the words, who is eager to have the goodwill of the audience on his side rather than have their resentment fighting against him, who wants also to have a

μᾶλλον ἢ τὸν φθόνον ἀνταγωνιστήν, ἔτι δὲ καὶ τὴν γνώμην εὔλυτον καὶ τὴν μνήμην εὔπορον καὶ τὴν λήθην ἄδηλον καθεστάναι βούλεται, καὶ τῇ χρείᾳ τοῦ βίου σύμμετρον τὴν δύναμιν τῶν λόγων κεκτῆσθαι πρόθυμός ἐστιν, οὐκ εἰκότως ἂν τοῦ μὲν αὐτοσχεδιάζειν ἀεί τε καὶ διὰ παντὸς ἐνεργὸν τὴν μελέτην ποιοῖτο, τοῦ δὲ γράφειν ἐν παιδιᾷ καὶ παρέργῳ ἐπιμελόμενος εὖ φρονεῖν κριθείη παρὰ τοῖς εὖ φρονοῦσιν;

ΟΔΥΣΣΕΥΣ
ΚΑΤΑ ΠΑΛΑΜΗΔΟΥΣ ΠΡΟΔΟΣΙΑΣ

(1) πολλάκις ἤδη ἐνεθυμήθην καὶ ἐθαύμασα, ὦ ἄνδρες Ἕλληνες, τὰς γνώμας τῶν λεγόντων, τί ποτε ἄρα βουλόμενοι ῥᾳδίως δεῦρο παριόντες συμβουλεύουσιν ὑμῖν, ἀφ᾽ ὧν ὠφέλεια μὲν οὐδεμία ἐστὶ τῷ κοινῷ, λοιδορίαι δὲ πλεῖσται γίγνονται ἐν ἀλλήλοις, εἰκῇ τε λόγους ἀναλίσκουσιν ἀκαίρους, περὶ ὧν ἂν τύχωσι. (2) λέγουσι δὲ τὴν αὐτῶν δόξαν ἕκαστος βουλόμενοί τι λαβεῖν, οἱ δὲ καὶ μισθὸν πραττόμενοι συναγορεύουσι, παρ᾽ ὁποτέρων ἂν νομίζωσι πλείω λήψεσθαι. καὶ εἰ μέν τις ἐν τῷ στρατοπέδῳ πλημμελεῖ ἢ βλάπτει τὸ κοινὸν χρήματα ἑαυτῷ ποριζόμενος, τούτων <ὁρῶ>μεν μηδένα τὸν φροντίζοντα εἶναι, εἰ δέ τις ἡμῶν αἰχμάλωτον ἀγαγὼν ἐκ τῶν πολεμίων τι γέρας εἴληφε πλέον ἕτερος ἑτέρου, τούτων ἕνεκα μεγάλας διαφορὰς ἐν ἡμῖν αὐτοῖς ἔχομεν διὰ τὰς τούτων σπουδάς. (3) ἐγὼ δὲ ἡγοῦμαι τὸν ἄνδρα τὸν ἀγαθὸν καὶ δίκαιον μήτε ἔχθρας ἰδίας φροντίζειν μήτε φιλεταιρίαν, φιλοτιμίᾳ χαρισάμενον ἕνεκα ἀνδρὸς ἑνός, <ἢ> χρήματα περὶ πλείονος ποιήσεσθαι, καὶ μὴ ὅ τι ἂν μέλλῃ τῷ πλήθει συνοίσειν. < .... >οὐ μὲν δὴ< .... > ἀλλὰ παραλιπὼν τοὺς ἀρχαίους πόνους τε καὶ λόγους πειράσομαι

flexible mind and a well-stocked and ready memory with no trace of forget-fulness, and who is keen to acquire an ability to make speeches which correspond to the needs of life, would he not, if he were to devote hard practice to extempore speaking all the time and in every circumstance, paying attention to writing for amusement and as a side-line, be properly reckoned by those who have good judgement to have good judgement too ?

Odysseus

Against the treachery of Palamedes

(1) Often in the past, men of Greece, I have pondered and been astonished at the intentions of those who address us, wondering what on earth their purpose is in readily coming forward here and giving advice to you when they offer no help to the common cause, and very many mutual insults are produced, and they waste untimely words at random on whatever subject they happen to choose. (2) They speak, each of them wanting to get some advantage in selfish glory, and some even charge a fee for consulting with those from whom they think they can get a greater return. And, if anyone in the camp sows discord or harms the common good by arranging things for himself, we see that none of these people cares. But if one of us in taking a prisoner from the enemy has obtained a prize which is bigger than that of someone else, this becomes the reason for us having great arguments amongst ourselves, thanks to their efforts. (3) But I think that the good, just man does not concern himself with personal enmity, nor does he set more store by favouritism, gratifying ambition for the sake of one man, nor by money, rather than by what is going to be to the advantage of the majority < .... >. But, leaving aside old troubles and arguments I will try to put this

Παλαμήδη τόνδε ἐν ὑμῖν εἰς κρίσιν δικαίως καταστῆσαι. (4) ἔστι δὲ τὸ πρᾶγμα, ὡς ἂν εἰδῆτε, προδοσία, ἐφ᾽ ᾗ δεκαπλάσιαι ζημίαι τῶν ἄλλων εἰσὶν ἐπικείμεναι, καίτοι, ὡς ὑμεῖς ἴστε πάντες, ἐμοὶ καὶ τούτῳ οὐδεμία πώποτ᾽ ἔχθρα οὐδ᾽ ἔρις ἐνεγένετο περὶ οὐδενὸς χρήματος, καὶ μὴν οὐδ᾽ ἐν παλαίστρᾳ οὐδ᾽ ἐν συμποσίῳ, ἔνθα φιλεῖ ἔριδας πλείστας καὶ λοιδορίας γίγνεσθαι. ὁ δὲ ἀνήρ ἐστι φιλόσοφός τε καὶ δεινός, οὗ μέλλω κατηγορεῖν, ὥστε εἰκότως τὸν νοῦν προσέχειν < δεῖν > ὑμᾶς καὶ μὴ ἀμελῆσαι περὶ τῶν νυνὶ λεγομένων.

(5) σχεδὸν μὲν γὰρ ἴστε καὶ αὐτοί, ἐν οἵῳ κινδύνῳ ἐγενόμεθα, ὅτε ἡμῶν οἱ μὲν εἰς τὰς ναῦς καταπεφευγότες ἦσαν, οἱ δὲ εἰς τὰς τάφρους, ἐνέπιπτόν τε εἰς τὰς σκηνὰς οἱ πολέμιοι, πᾶσά τε ἀπορία ἦν, ποῖ ποτε προβήσοιτο ἡ τοῦ μέλλοντος κακοῦ τελευτή. < .... > ἔχει δὲ ὧδε ὑμῖν· ἐτυγχάνομεν πλησίον τῶν πυλῶν ἐν τῷ αὐτῷ συντασσόμενοι ἐγώ τε καὶ Διομήδης, πλησίον δ᾽ ἦν Παλαμήδης καὶ Πολυποίτης. (6) συνιόντων δὲ ἡμῶν ὁμόσε τοῖς ἀνδράσιν, ἐκδραμὼν τοξότης ἐκ τῶν πολεμίων ἐστοχάσατο τούτου, ἁμαρτὼν δὲ αὐτοῦ βάλλει ἐγγὺς ἐμοῦ· οὗτός τε λόγχην ἀφίησιν ἐπ᾽ αὐτόν, καὶ ἐκεῖνος ἀνελόμενος ᾤχετο εἰς τὸ στρατόπεδον. ἐγὼ δὲ ἀνελὼν τὸν οἰστὸν δίδωμι Εὐρυβάτῃ δοῦναι Τεύκρῳ, ἵνα χρῷτο. ἀνοχῆς δὲ γενομένης ἀπὸ τῆς μάχης ὀλίγον χρόνον, δείκνυσί μοι τὸν οἰστὸν ὑπὸ τοῖς πτεροῖς γράμματα ἔχοντα. (7) ἐκπλαγεὶς δὲ ἐγὼ τῷ πραγμάτι, προσκαλεσάμενος Σθένελόν τε καὶ Διομήδη ἐδείκνυον αὐτοῖς τὰ ἐνόντα. ἡ δὲ γραφὴ ἐδήλου τάδε· "Ἀλέξανδρος Παλαμήδει. ὅσα συνέθου Τηλέφῳ, πάντα σοι ἔσται, ὅ τε πατὴρ Κασάνδραν γυναῖκα δίδωσί σοι, καθάπερ ἐπέστειλας· ἀλλὰ τὰ ἀπὸ σοῦ πραττέσθω διὰ τάχους." ἐνεγέγραπτο μὲν ταῦτα· καί μοι προσελθόντες μαρτυρήσατε οἱ λαβόντες τὸ τόξευμα.

man Palamedes on trial before you fairly. (4) The fact of the matter, as you may be aware, is treachery; for this, punishments are prescribed which are ten times greater than for other crimes, and yet, as you all know, there has never been any hostility or quarrel between me and him on any matter up to now, and moreover this has been so both in the palaistra and in the drinking party where very many quarrels and insults begin. The man I am going to accuse is both educated and clever, so it is right that you must give me your attention and not be careless over what is now being said.

(5) For you yourselves are pretty well aware of what danger we were in when some of us had fled to the ships and others to the trenches and the enemy was falling on the tents and there was complete helplessness over what the outcome of the coming trouble could possibly be. < .... > there you have the situation. Diomedes and I happened to be near the gates, stationed together in the ranks in the same place, and Palamedes was close by with Polypoites. (6) And when we came to close quarters, an archer running out from the enemy took aim at this man and missing him hit the ground near me. Palamedes let fly his spear towards him and he, picking it up, went off to the camp. I picked up the arrow and gave it to Eurybates to give to Teukros so that he could use it. And, when there was a short pause in the battle, he showed me the arrow which had some writing under the feathers. (7) I, astounded at this business, summoned Sthenelos and Diomedes and showed them what was on it. The writing said this: "Alexandros to Palamedes. All that you agreed with Telephos will be yours and her father gives Cassandra to you as wife just as you ordered in your message. But let your side of things be done speedily." That is what had been written on it; let those who received the arrow come forward and bear witness on my behalf.

< WITNESSES >

< ΜΑΡΤΥΡΕΣ >

(8) ἐπέδειξα δὲ ἂν καὶ αὐτὸ τὸ τόξευμα ὑμῖν, ὡς ἀληθὲς ἦν·
νῦν δὲ ἐν τῷ θορύβῳ ἔλαθεν αὐτὸ Τεῦκρος ἀποτοξεύσας. δεῖ
δέ με καὶ τὰ λοιπὰ διελθεῖν, ὡς ἔχει, μηδ' εἰκῇ οὕτως ἄνδρα
σύμμαχον περὶ θανάτου κρίνειν, αἰσχίστην αἰτίαν
προστιθέντα καὶ ταῦτα πρότερον ἐν ὑμῖν εὐδοκιμηκότι. (9)
ἡμεῖς μὲν γὰρ πρὶν ἐμβαλεῖν δεῦρο πολὺν χρόνον ἐν ταὐτῷ
ἐγενόμεθα, καὶ οὐδεὶς ἡμῶν εἶδεν ἔχοντα τοῦτον σημεῖον ἐν
τῇ ἀσπίδι· ἐπειδὴ δὲ κατεπλεύσαμεν δεῦρο τρίαιναν
ἐπεγράψατο. τίνος ἕνεκα; ἵνα δῆλος εἴη τῷ ἐπιγράμματι, ὅ τε
ἀντιτεταγμένος τοῦτον τοξεύοι διὰ τὸ σύνθημα, οὗτός τε εἰς
ἐκεῖνον ἐσακοντίζοι. (10) τεκμαίρεσθαι δὲ δεῖ ἐκ τούτων
εἰκότως καὶ τὴν ἄφεσιν τῆς λόγχης. φημὶ γὰρ καὶ ἐν ἐκείνῃ
γράμματα εἶναι, πηνίκα τε καὶ πότε προδώσει· πιστὰ γὰρ ἦν
οὕτω παρ' ἀλλήλων τὰ πεμπόμενα, οὗτός τε ἐκείνοις ἐκείνοί
τε τούτῳ πέμποντες διὰ τοιούτου εἴδους καὶ μὴ δι' ἀγγέλων.
(11) ἔτι δὲ καὶ τόδε σκεψώμεθα. ψήφισμα ἡμῖν ἐγένετο, ὃς ἂν
βέλος τι λάβῃ ἐκ τῶν πολεμίων, ἀποφέρειν πρὸς τοὺς
ἡγεμόνας διὰ τὸ σπανίοις αὐτοῖς χρῆσθαι ἡμᾶς· καὶ οἱ μὲν
ἄλλοι πειθαρχοῦσι τοῖς ἐψηφισμένοις, οὗτος δὲ βέλη
ἀνελόμενος πέντε φανερός ἐστιν οὐδὲ ἓν πρὸς ὑμᾶς ἐνηνοχώς,
ὥστε καὶ διὰ ταῦτα δικαίως ἄν μοι δοκεῖ θανάτῳ
ζημιωθῆναι. (12) ἆρά γε ἐνθυμεῖσθε, ὦ ἄνδρες Ἕλληνες, ὅτι
ταῦτα τοῦ σοφιστοῦ τῆς διανοίας καὶ τοῦ φρονήματος
αὐτοῦ < .... >, ὃς τυγχάνει φιλοσοφῶν ἐφ' οἷς ἥκιστα ἐχρῆν
αὐτὸν ταῦτα πράττειν; τά τε πράγματα τὰ περιεστηκότα καὶ
τὴν στρατείαν πᾶσαν ἐπιδείξω αἴτιον γεγονότα ἡμῖν τόν τε
πατέρα αὐτοῦ καὶ τοῦτον αὐτόν. ἀνάγκη δὲ καὶ διὰ
μακροτέρων λόγων ῥηθῆναι τὰ γενόμενα.

τούτῳ πατήρ ἐστι πένης, ὄνομα Ναύπλιος, τέχνην ἔχων

(8) And I would have shown you the very arrow to show that this was true; but, as it was, in the confusion Teukros shot it back without realizing it. And I must give an account of how the remaining matters stand too, and not judge a fellow-soldier thus lightly on a capital charge, putting forward a most shameful accusation and that against someone who has previously enjoyed a good reputation among you. (9) For, before we made our invasion here, we were in the same place for a long time and none of us saw him with a sign on his shield. But, when we sailed here, he had a trident embossed on it. For what purpose ? So that he might be identifiable because of the design, and so that his opposite number might fire an arrow towards him according to the agreement and he might throw his javelin at him. (10) We must also make a probable inference from these things about the hurling of the javelin too. For I say that on that also there was writing to say at what hour and when he would commit his treachery. For it was thus that what was sent by both parties was authenticated, this man sending to them and they to him in such a manner and not by messengers. (11) Yet let us also look at this. We had a decree that whoever captured any weapon from the enemy should take it to the generals since we had a shortage; and, whereas the others abided by the terms of the decree, this man, having picked up five weapons, clearly brought not even one of them to you, so that, for this reason too, it seems to me that he should justly be punished with death. (12) Do you consider, men of Greece, that these things < .... > the intent and thinking of this expert who happens to be using his ingenuity in those matters in which he should least of all have acted ? And I shall demonstrate that his father and he himself are responsible for our present circumstances and for the whole expedition. It is necessary that what has happened should be explained at greater length.

He has a father who is a poor man, called Nauplios, a fisherman by trade.

ἁλιείαν. (13) οὗτος πλείστους τῶν Ἑλλήνων ἠφάνικε, χρήματά τε πολλὰ ἐκ τῶν νεῶν ὑφῄρηται, κακά τε πλεῖστα τοὺς ναυτίλους εἴργασται, πανουργίας τε οὐδεμιᾶς λείπεται· γνώσεσθε δὲ προϊόντος τοῦ λόγου, τὰς ἀληθείας ἀκούσαντες τῶν γενομένων. (14) Ἀλέῳ γὰρ τῷ Τεγέας βασιλεῖ ἀφικομένῳ εἰς Δελφοὺς ἐχρήσθη ὑπὸ τοῦ θεοῦ, ὅτι αὐτῷ ἔκγονος ἐκ τῆς θυγατρὸς εἰ γένοιτο, ὑπὸ τούτου δεῖν τοὺς υἱοὺς αὐτοῦ ἀπολέσθαι. ἀκούσας δὲ ταῦτα ὁ Ἄλεος διὰ τάχους ἀφικνεῖται οἴκαδε, καὶ καθίστησι τὴν θυγατέρα ἱέρειαν τῆς Ἀθηνᾶς, εἰπών, εἴ ποτε ἀνδρὶ συγγενήσεται, θανατώσειν αὐτήν. τύχης δὲ γενομένης ἀφικνεῖται Ἡρακλῆς στρατευόμενος ἐπ' Αὐγέαν εἰς Ἦλιν, καὶ αὐτὸν ξενίζει ὁ Ἄλεος ἐν τῷ ἱερῷ τῆς Ἀθηνᾶς. (15) ἰδὼν δὲ ὁ Ἡρακλῆς τὴν παῖδα ἐν τῷ νεῷ ὑπὸ μέθης συνεγένετο. ἐπεὶ δὲ κύουσαν αὐτὴν ὁ πατὴρ ἤσθετο Ἄλεος, μεταπέμπεται τὸν τούτου πατέρα, πυθόμενος πορθμέα τε εἶναι αὐτὸν καὶ δεινόν. ἀφικομένου δὲ τοῦ Ναυπλίου δίδωσιν αὐτῷ τὴν παῖδα καταποντίσαι. (16) ὃ δὲ παραλαβὼν ἦγεν αὐτήν, καὶ ὡς γίγνονται ἐν τῷ Παρθενίῳ ὄρει, τίκτει Τήλεφον. ἀμελήσας δὲ ὧν ὁ Ἄλεος αὐτῷ ἐπέστειλεν, ἄγων αὐτὴν ἀπέδοτο καὶ τὸ παιδίον ἐς Μυσίαν Τεύθραντι τῷ βασιλεῖ. ὁ δὲ Τεύθρας ἄπαις ὢν τὴν μὲν Αὔγην γυναῖκα ποιεῖται, τὸν δὲ παῖδα αὐτῆς ἐπονομάσας Τήλεφον τίθεται υἱὸν ἑαυτοῦ, δίδωσί ϛε Πριάμῳ αὐτὸν εἰς τὸ Ἴλιον παιδεῦσαι. (17) χρόνου δὲ προϊόντος Ἀλέξανδρος ἐπεθύμησεν εἰς τὴν Ἑλλάδ' ἀφικέσθαι, τό τε ἱερὸν τὸ ἐν Δελφοῖς θεωρῆσαι βουλόμενος, ἅμα δὲ καὶ τὸ κάλλος τῆς Ἑλένης ἀκούων δηλονότι, καὶ τὴν τοῦ Τηλέφου γένεσιν ἀκηκοώς, ὁπόθεν τε εἴη καὶ τίνα τρόπον καὶ ὑπὸ τίνος ἐπράθη. ὥστε Ἀλέξανδρος οὕτω τὴν ἀποδημίαν ἐποιεῖτο διὰ προφάσεις τοιαύτας εἰς τὴν Ἑλλάδα. ἐν δὲ τῷ καιρῷ τούτῳ οἱ Μόλου παῖδες ἀφικνοῦνται ἐκ Κρήτης, δεόμενοι Μενέλεω αὐτούς τε διαλλάξαι καὶ διελεῖν

(13) This man has eliminated large numbers of Greeks, stolen many goods from their ships, done very great violence to the sailors and left no kind of crime untouched. And, as my speech goes on, you will realize this as you hear the truth of what happened. (14) When Aleos, king of Tegea, came to Delphi, he received a prophecy from the god that, if his daughter had offspring, it was inevitable that his sons would die at the hands of this person. On hearing this Aleos quickly came home and appointed his daughter as a priestess of Athena, telling her that, if she ever had intercourse with a man, she would be put to death. And, as chance would have it, Herakles arrived on his expedition against Augeas going towards Elis, and Aleos gave him hospitality in the temple of Athena. (15) Herakles, seeing the young girl, had intercourse with her in the temple, drink being to blame. When her father Aleos realized that she was pregnant, he sent for Palamedes' father since he had discovered that he was a boatman and a good one too. When Nauplios arrived, he gave him the girl to drown in the sea. (16) But he, on receiving her, took her away and, when they were on Mount Parthenion, she gave birth to Telephos. Neglecting the orders which Aleos had given him, he brought the girl and the baby to Mysia and sold them to King Teuthras. And, since Teuthras was childless, he made Auge his wife and, having given the child the name Telephos, he made him his son and gave him to Priam to educate, sending him to Troy. (17) As time went on, Alexandros had a desire to visit Greece, both wanting to see the temple at Delphi (at the same time, of course, having word of Helen's beauty too) and having heard of the birth of Telephos – where he had come from and how and by whom he was sold. So it was on such pretexts that Alexandros made his excursion to Greece. And at this critical moment the children of Molos arrived from Crete asking Menelaus

τὴν κτῆσιν αὐτοῖς, ὅτι εἴη ὁ πατὴρ τετελευτηκὼς αὐτοί τε
στασιάζοιεν περὶ τῶν πατρῴων χρημάτων. (18) εἶεν· τί οὖν
γίγνεται; πλεῖν αὐτῷ ἔδοξε, καὶ ἐπιστείλας τῇ γυναικὶ καὶ
τοῖς ἀδελφοῖς < αὐτῆς > ἐπιμελεῖσθαι τῶν ξένων, ἵνα μηδενὸς
ἔσοιντο ἐνδεεῖς, ἕως ἂν αὐτὸς ἔλθῃ ἐκ Κρήτης, ὁ μὲν ᾤχετο·
Ἀλέξανδρος δὲ αὐτοῦ τὴν γυναῖκα ἐξαπατήσας, ἐκ τῶν
οἴκων λαβὼν ὅσα πλεῖστα ἐδύνατο, ἀποπλέων ᾤχετο, οὐκ
αἰδεσθεὶς οὔτε Δία ξένιον οὔτε θεῶν οὐδένα, ἄνομα καὶ
βάρβαρα ἔργα διαπραξάμενος, ἄπιστα πᾶσι καὶ τοῖς
ἐπιγιγνομένοις ἀκοῦσαι. (19) ἀποιχομένου δὲ αὐτοῦ πάλιν εἰς
Ἀσίαν, ἄγοντος τὰ χρήματα καὶ τὴν γυναῖκα, ἔστιν ὅπου
ἀντελάβου τινὸς ἢ βοῇ ἐσήμηνας τοῖς περιοίκοις ἢ βοήθειαν
συνέλεξας; οὐκ ἂν ἔχοις εἰπεῖν, ἀλλὰ περιεῖδες Ἕλληνας ὑπὸ
βαρβάρων ὑβρισθέντας. (20) ἐπεὶ δὲ ἐπύθοντο οἱ Ἕλληνες
τὴν ἁρπαγὴν καὶ Μενέλεως ᾔσθετο, ἤγειρε τὴν στρατιὰν καὶ
διέπεμπεν ἡμῶν ἄλλον ἄλλοσε εἰς τὰς πόλεις αἰτήσων τὰς
στρατιάς. καὶ δὴ τοῦτον ἔπεμψεν εἰς Χίον πρὸς Οἰνοπίωνα
καὶ εἰς Κύπρον πρὸς Κινύραν. ὁ δὲ < .... > Κινύραν τε ἔπεισε
μὴ συστρατεύειν ἡμῖν, δῶρά τε πολλὰ παρ᾽ αὐτοῦ λαβὼν
ἀποπλέων ᾤχετο. (21) καὶ Ἀγαμέμνονι μὲν ἀποδίδωσι
χαλκοῦν θώρακα, ὅστις οὐδενὸς ἄξιος ἦν, τὰ δὲ ἄλλα αὐτὸς
ἔχει χρήματα. ἀπήγγελλε δὲ ὅτι ἑκατὸν ναῦς ἀποπέμψει ὁ
Κινύρας· ὁρᾶτε δὲ καὶ αὐτοὶ οὐδεμίαν παρ᾽ αὐτοῦ ἤκουσαν.
ὥστε καὶ διὰ ταῦτα δικαίως ἄν μοι δοκεῖ θανάτῳ
ζημιωθῆναι, εἰ ἄρα γε κολάσασθαι ἄξιόν ἐστι τὸν
σοφιστήν, ὃς ἐπὶ τοῖς φίλοις τὰ αἴσχιστα μηχανώμενος
πέφανται.

(22) ἄξιον δὲ καταμαθεῖν, ἃ καὶ φιλοσοφεῖν ἐπικεχείρηκεν
ἐξαπατῶν τοὺς νέους καὶ παραπείθων, φάσκων τάξεις
ἐξευρηκέναι πολεμικάς, γράμματα, ἀριθμούς, μέτρα,
σταθμούς, πεττούς, κύβους, μουσικήν, νόμισμα, πυρσούς. καὶ

to reconcile them and divide their property for them because their father had died and they themselves were quarrelling about their father's goods. (18) Well, so what happens? Menelaus decided to sail and, having ordered his wife and her brothers to look after the guests, seeing that they should not want for anything until he himself should return from Crete, he departed. But Alexandros, having deceived Menelaus' wife and having taken as much as he could from her home, went off and sailed away, respecting neither Zeus, the god of guests, nor any of the gods, having committed lawless and barbarous deeds incredible to everyone, including those in subsequent ages. (19) And, when he was leaving to return to Asia with the goods and the lady, did you on any occasion get hold of anyone or shout to give an alarm to the neighbours or assemble help ? You could have nothing to say, but you stood by and watched Greeks being insulted by barbarians. (20) When the Greeks and Menelaus discovered the theft, Menelaus got together an expedition and sent many of us in different directions to the cities to ask for troops. Indeed he sent this man to Oinopion in Chios and to Kinyras in Cyprus. But he < .... > and persuaded Kinyras not to join us on the expedition and left there on his ship taking many presents from Kinyras. (21) And he gave a bronze breastplate to Agamemnon which was worth nothing and he himself held on to the other goods. And he reported that Kinyras would send one hundred ships – you yourselves see that not one has come from him. So, on this account too, it seems to me that death would be a just punishment for him, if indeed it is just to punish this expert who has been shown to be devising the most disgraceful things against his friends.

(22) And it is worth carefully considering in what matters he tried to be clever, deceiving the young and inveigling them into believing his assertions that he had invented formations for war, letters, numbers, measures, weights, draughts, dice, music, coinage and fire-beacons. And he does not even feel

οὐδὲ αἰσχύνεται, ὅταν αὐτίκα ἐλέγχηται φανερῶς ἐν ὑμῖν ψευδόμενος. (23) Νέστωρ γὰρ ὅδ᾽ ὁ πρεσβύτατος ἡμῶν ἁπάντων καὶ αὐτὸς ἐν τοῖς Πειρίθου γάμοις μετὰ Λαπιθῶν ἐμαχέσατο Κενταύροις ἐν φάλαγγι καὶ τάξει· Μενεσθεὺς δὲ πρῶτος λέγεται κοσμῆσαι τάξεις καὶ λόχους καὶ φάλαγγας συστῆσαι, ἡνίκα Εὔμολπος ὁ Ποσειδῶνος ἐπ᾽ Ἀθηναίους ἐστράτευσε Θρᾷκας ἄγων· ὥστ᾽ οὐ Παλαμήδους τὸ ἐξεύρημά ἐστιν, ἀλλ᾽ ἄλλων πρότερον. (24) γράμματα μὲν δὴ πρῶτος Ὀρφεὺς ἐξήνεγκε, παρὰ Μουσῶν μαθών, ὡς καὶ ἐπὶ τῷ μνήματι αὐτοῦ δηλοῖ τὰ ἐπιγράμματα·

> Μουσάων πρόπολον τῇδ᾽ Ὀρφέα Θρῆκες ἔθηκαν,
> ὃν κτάνεν ὑψιμέδων Ζεὺς ψολόεντι βέλει
> Οἰάγρου φίλον υἱόν, ὃς Ἡρακλῆ᾽ ἐδίδαξεν,
> εὑρὼν ἀνθρώποις γράμματα καὶ σοφίην.

(25) μουσικὴν δὲ Λίνος ὁ Καλλιόπης, ὃν Ἡρακλῆς φονεύει. ἀριθμούς γε μὴν Μουσαῖος ὁ τῶν Εὐμολπιδῶν, Ἀθηναῖος, ὡς καὶ τὰ ποιήματα αὐτοῦ δηλοῖ·

> ὄρθιον ἑξαμερὲς τετόρων καὶ εἴκοσι μέτρων.
> ὡς δεκάτην γενέην ἑκατὸν βιοτευέμεν ἄνδρας.

(26) νομίσματα δὲ οὐ Φοίνικες ἐξεῦρον, λογιώτατοι καὶ δεινότατοι ὄντες τῶν βαρβάρων; ἐξ ὁλοσφύρου γὰρ ἴσον μερισμὸν διείλοντο, καὶ πρῶτοι χαρακτῆρα ἔβαλον, εἰς τὸν σταθμὸν < .... > τὸ πλέον καὶ τὸ ἔλαττον. παρ᾽ ὧν οὗτος ἐλθὼν σοφίζεται τὸν αὐτὸν ῥυθμόν. ὥστε αὐτοῦ ταῦτα πάντα πρεσβύτερα φαίνεται, ὧν οὗτος προσποιεῖται εὑρετὴς εἶναι. (27) μέτρα δὲ καὶ σταθμὰ ἐξεῦρε καπήλοις καὶ ἀγοραίοις ἀνθρώποις ἀπάτας καὶ ἐπιορκίας, πεττούς γε μὴν τοῖς ἀργοῖς τῶν ἀνδρῶν ἔριδας καὶ λοιδορίας. καὶ κύβους αὖ μέγιστον

shame when he is straightway found out to be openly lying in your company. (23) For Nestor here, the oldest of us all, himself fought alongside the Lapiths against the Centaurs at the marriage of Peirithoos in a phalanx-formation; and Menestheus is said to have been the first to dispose formations and companies and to have formed phalanxes when Eumolpos, son of Poseidon, made an expedition against the Athenians, taking Thracians with him. So it is not Palamcdes' invention but that of others before him. (24) Orpheus was the first to introduce writing, having learnt it from the Muses, as the inscription on his tomb shows:

> The Thracians buried Orpheus here, the minister of the Muses
>
> Whom lofty-ruling Zeus slew with the smoking thunderbolt
>
> The dear son of Oiagros, who taught Herakles
>
> Having discovered writing and wisdom for mankind.

(25) And Linos, son of Kalliope, whom Herakles killed, discovered music, and furthermore Mousaios, son of the Eumolpidai, an Athenian, discovered numbers as his poems too show:

> A straight hexameter of four and twenty measures.
>
> So that a hundred men live as a tenth generation.

(26) Did not the Phoenicians, being the most logical and clever of the barbarians, discover coinage? They divided a beaten ingot into equal parts and first struck the die < .... > greater or lesser value according to weight. And following these this man comes and makes himself clever after the same pattern. So all these things of which he claims to be the inventor are older than him. (27) He discovered measures and weights for traders and men of the market-place to be sources of deceit and perjury, and draughts for the lazy ones, which produce quarrels and insults. And again he invented dice, a very great evil giving pain and penalty to the losers and mockery and reproach to

κακὸν κατέδειξε, τοῖς μὲν ἡττηθεῖσι λύπας καὶ ζημίας, τοῖς δὲ νενικηκόσι καταγέλωτα καὶ ὄνειδος· τὰ γὰρ ἀπὸ τῶν κύβων προσγιγνόμενα ἀνόνητα γίγνεται, τὰ δὲ πλεῖστα καταναλίσκεται παραχρῆμα. (28) πυρσοὺς αὖ ἐσοφίσατο, ἀλλ' ἐπὶ τῷ ἡμετέρῳ κακῷ { ἃ } διενοεῖτο ποιεῖν, χρήσιμον δὲ τοῖς πολεμίοις. ἀρετὴ δέ ἐστιν ἀνδρὸς τοῖς ἡγεμόσι προσέχειν καὶ τὸ προσταττόμενον ποιεῖν καὶ τῷ πλήθει ἀρέσκειν παντί, αὑτόν τε παρέχειν ἄνδρα πανταχοῦ ἀγαθόν, τούς τε φίλους εὖ ποιοῦντα καὶ τοὺς ἐχθροὺς κακῶς. ὧν τἀναντία πάντων οὗτος ἐπίσταται, τοὺς μὲν ἐχθροὺς ὠφελεῖν, τοὺς δὲ φίλους κακῶς ποιεῖν.

(29) ἀξιῶ δ' ὑμᾶς ἔγωγε κοινῇ σκεψαμένους βουλεύσασθαι περὶ αὐτοῦ καὶ μὴ ἀφεῖναι αὐτὸν ὑποχείριον λαβόντας. εἰ δὲ κατελεήσαντες αὐτὸν διὰ τὸν δεινότητα τῶν λόγων ἀφήσετε, θαυμαστὴ παρανομία γενήσεται ἐν τῷ στρατεύματι· εἰδὼς γὰρ αὐτῶν ἕκαστος ὅτι καὶ Παλαμήδης περιφανῶς τοσαῦτα ἡμαρτηκὼς οὐδεμίαν δίκην ἔδωκε, καὶ αὐτοὶ πειράσονται ἀδικεῖν. ὥστε ἐὰν νοῦν ἔχητε, ψηφιεῖσθε τὰ βέλτιστ' ὑμῖν αὐτοῖς, καὶ τῶν λοιπῶν οὕνεκα παράδειγμα ποιήσεσθε τοῦτον τιμωρησάμενοι.

THE FRAGMENTS

ΜΕΣΣΗΝΙΑΚΟΣ

1. ἐλευθέρους ἀφῆκε πάντας θεός· οὐδένα δοῦλον ἡ φύσις πεποίηκεν.

2. εἰ γὰρ ὁ πόλεμος αἴτιος τῶν παρόντων κακῶν, μετὰ τῆς εἰρήνης δεῖ ἐπανορθώσασθαι.

the winners. For the proceeds of dice bring no benefits and most of them are spent straightaway. (28) Fire-beacons again he devised, but he intended to make them for our detriment and as something useful to the enemy. It is the virtue of man to give heed to leaders and to do what is commanded and to please the whole host and to present oneself everywhere as a good man, doing well by friends and ill by enemies. This man knows about the opposite of all this, helping enemies and doing ill to friends.

(29) I believe that you, looking at this together with me, should consider his case and not let him go when you have him in your hands. And if, having felt sorry for him, you let him off because of the cleverness of his arguments, an astonishing lack of discipline in the army will ensue. For each of the troops, knowing that Palamedes too has paid no penalty when he has openly done wrong in so many ways, will try to do wrong themselves. So, if you are sensible, you will vote for what is best for you, and, for the sake of others, make an example of this man by punishing him.

THE FRAGMENTS

THE MESSENIAN SPEECH

1. God has given all men their freedom; nature has made no man a slave.

2. For if war is the cause of present woes, with peace must they be righted.

ΑΜΦΙΣΒΗΤΗΣΙΜΑ

3. πάντες τοὺς σοφοὺς τιμῶσιν· Πάριοι γοῦν Ἀρχίλοχον καίπερ βλάσφημον ὄντα τετιμήκασι, καὶ Χῖοι Ὅμηρον οὐκ ὄντα πολίτην, καὶ Μυτιληναῖοι Σαπφὼ καίπερ γυναῖκα οὖσαν, καὶ Λακεδαιμόνιοι Χείλωνα καὶ τῶν γερόντων ἐποίησαν ἥκιστα φιλόλογοι ὄντες, καὶ Λαμψακηνοὶ Ἀναξαγόραν ξένον ὄντα ἔθαψαν καὶ τιμῶσιν ἔτι καὶ νῦν.

4. Ἀθηναῖοι τοῖς Σόλωνος νόμοις χρησάμενοι εὐδαιμόνησαν καὶ Λακεδαιμόνιοι τοῖς Λυκούργου, καὶ Θήβησιν ἅμα οἱ προστάται φιλόσοφοι ἐγένοντο καὶ εὐδαιμόνησεν ἡ πόλις.

ΡΗΤΟΡΙΚΑ

5. Ἀλκιδάμας δὲ τεττάρας λόγους φησί· φάσιν, ἀπόφασιν, ἐρώτησιν, προσαγόρευσιν.

6. ἡ διαλεκτικὴ οὕτως ὁρίζεται·
... δύναμις τοῦ ὄντος πιθανοῦ.

ΑΡΙΣΤΟΤΕΛΗΣ – ΡΗΤΟΡΙΚΑ Γ

7. μένους μὲν τὴν ψυχὴν πληρουμένην, πυρίχρων δὲ τὴν ὄψιν γινομένην.

8. τελεσφόρον ᾠήθη τὴν προθυμίαν αὐτῶν γενήσεσθαι.

9. τελεσφόρον τὴν πειθὼ τῶν λόγων κατέστησεν.

QUOTATIONS OF DOUBTFUL ORIGIN

3. All honour the wise; at any rate, the Parians have honoured Archilochus although he is irreverent, and the Chians Homer although he is not one of their citizens, and the Mytileneans Sappho although she is a woman, and the Spartans even made Chilon one of their elders although they are not in the least literary-minded, and the people of Lampsacus gave burial to Anaxagoras who was a foreigner and they honour him even to this day.

4. The Athenians prospered when they adopted Solon's laws and so did the Spartans with the laws of Lycurgus, and the rulers of Thebes became philosophers and simultaneously the city prospered.

RHETORICAL WRITINGS

5. Alcidamas says there are four forms of language: assertion, denial, question and address.

6. Dialectic is thus defined: .... the capacity for persuasion.

ARISTOTLE - *RHETORIC* Book iii

7. .... the soul being filled with rage, and the face becoming the colour of fire.

8. He thought their enthusiasm would accomplish its end.

9. He made the persuasiveness of speeches accomplish its end.

10. κυανόχρων τὸ τῆς θαλάττης ἔδαφος.

11. οὐδὲν τοιοῦτον ἄθυρμα τῇ ποιήσει προσφέρων.

12. τὴν τῆς φύσεως ἀτασθαλίαν.

13. ἀκράτῳ τῆς διανοίας ὀργῇ τεθηγμένον.

14. τὸν ὑγρὸν ἱδρῶτα.

15. εἰς τὴν τῶν Ἰσθμίων πανήγυριν.

16. τοὺς τῶν πόλεων βασιλεῖς νόμους.

17. δρομαίᾳ τῇ τῆς ψυχῆς ὁρμῇ.

18. τὸ τῆς φύσεως παραλαβὼν μουσεῖον.

19. σκυθρωπὸν τὴν φροντίδα τῆς ψυχῆς.

20. πανδήμου χάριτος δημιουργὸς καὶ οἰκονόμος τῆς τῶν ἀκουόντων ἡδονῆς.

21. τοῖς τῆς ὕλης κλάδοις τὴν τοῦ σώματος αἰσχύνην παρήμπισχεν.

22. ἀντίμιμον τὴν τῆς ψυχῆς ἐπιθυμίαν.

23. ἔξεδρον τὴν τῆς μοχθηρίας ὑπερβολήν.

24. φιλοσοφία .... ἐπιτείχισμα τῶν νόμων.

10. .... dark-hued is the bottom of the sea.

11. .... bringing no such plaything to his poetry.

12. .... the recklessness of nature.

13. .... whetted with the pure rage of his intellect.

14. .... damp sweat.

15. .... to the concourse of the Isthmian Games.

16. .... the laws, the kings of cities.

17. .... with a runner's eagerness of soul.

18. .... having taken over the museum of nature.

19. .... scowling was his anxious soul.

20. .... the craftsman of universal popularity and the steward of his audience's pleasure.

21. He clothed the embarrassment of his body with branches of wood.

22. .... the desire of the soul imitating in return.

23. .... extravagant the excess of wickedness.

24. .... philosophy, the bulwark of the laws.

25. Ὀδύσσεια .... καλὸν ἀνθρωπίνου βίου κάτοπτρον.

[ΜΟΥΣΕΙΟΝ]

26. ἀρχὴν μὲν μὴ φῦναι ἐπιχθονίοισιν ἄριστον,
    φύντα δ᾽ ὅπως ὤκιστα πύλας Ἀίδαο περῆσαι.

ΠΕΡΙ ΟΜΗΡΟΥ

27. οἱ δὲ ὁρῶντες αὐτὸν ἐσχεδίασαν τόνδε τὸν στίχον·
    ὅσσ᾽ ἕλομεν λιπόμεσθ᾽, ὅσσ᾽ οὐχ ἕλομεν φερόμεσθα.
ὁ δὲ οὐ δυνάμενος εὑρεῖν τὸ λεχθὲν ἤρετο αὐτοὺς ὅ τι
λέγοιεν. οἱ δὲ ἔφασαν ἐφ᾽ ἁλιείαν οἰχόμενοι ἀγρεῦσαι μὲν
οὐδέν, καθήμενοι δὲ φθειρίζεσθαι, τῶν δὲ φθειρῶν οὓς ἔλαβον
αὐτοῦ καταλιπεῖν, οὓς δ᾽ οὐκ ἔλαβον ἐν τοῖς τρίβωσιν ἐν[θ]᾽
ἀποφέρειν. ἀναμνησθεὶς δὲ τοῦ μαντείου, ὅτι ἡ καταστροφὴ
αὐτῷ τοῦ βίου ἧκεν, ποιεῖ εἰς ἑαυτὸν ἐπίγραμμα τόδε·
    ἐνθάδε τὴν ἱερὴν κεφαλὴν κατὰ γαῖα κάλυψε
    ἀνδρῶν ἡρώων κοσμήτορα θεῖον Ὅμηρον.
καὶ ἀναχωρῶν πηλοῦ ὄντος ὀλισθάνει καὶ πεσὼν ἐπὶ
πλευρὰν οὕτως, φασίν, ἐτελεύτησεν. περὶ δὲ τούτου μὲν οὖν
ποιεῖσθαι τὴν ἀρετὴν πειρασόμεθα, μάλιστα δ᾽ ὁρῶντες τοὺς
ἱστορικοὺς θαυμαζομένους. Ὅμηρος γοῦν διὰ τοῦτο καὶ ζῶν
καὶ ἀποθανὼν τετίμηται παρὰ πᾶσιν ἀνθρώποις. ταύτη[ν]
οὖν αὐτῷ τῆς παιδιᾶς χάριν ἀποδίδο[ντες τὸ γέ]νος αὐτοῦ
καὶ τὴν ἄλλην ποίησιν δι᾽ ἀκ[ριβ]είας μνήμης τοῖς βουλομένοις φι[λοκαλ]εῖν τῶν Ἑλλήνων εἰς τὸ κοινὸν παραδῶμεν.
                    Ἀλκι]δάμαντος
                    περὶ Ὁμήρου

25. .... the *Odyssey* .... a fine mirror of human life.

[THE MOUSEION]

26.   To begin, it is best not to be born with those upon the earth,

But, being born, to pass the gates of Hades as swiftly as you may.

ON HOMER

27. And they, seeing him, improvised this line:

What we took we left, what we did not take we carried away.

But he, being unable to discover the meaning of what they said, asked them what they were talking about. They replied that they had gone fishing, but, having caught nothing, sat down and started to pick lice from themselves, and those they caught they left there, but those they did not catch they took away in their cloaks. Remembering the prophecy that the end of his life had come, he composed this epigram for himself:

Here earth hides the sacred head

Of godlike Homer who marshalled heroes.

And, as he was returning, he slipped since it was muddy, and, having fallen on his side, thus, they say, he made his end. On this subject, then, we shall try to make our reputation, especially since we see the admiration given to writers of history. Homer, at least, because of this, both in life and death has been honoured by all men. So, publishing this to thank him for his entertainment, let us with precise recollection hand down the story of his birth and the rest of his poetry to those Greeks who aspire to cultivated taste.

Alcidamas

On Homer

Commentary

On those who write written speeches
or
On sophists

1 – 4

Some of those called sophists, who have no more qualification for the task of speech-making than ordinary people, are giving themselves airs, claiming they are masters of rhetoric when they have only acquired part of the craft, namely the skill of script-writing. In spending their time on this they reveal serious short-comings in both professional skill and general culture. I can write texts but I believe that writing texts should be a subordinate, additional activity for the speech-maker. Taking time over writing and making good use of past practice is easy even for the untrained.

The introduction sets out the central point which Alcidamas will elaborate in the rest of the treatise. The context is clearly that of rivalry between teachers of rhetoric in a period of rapid development for a new discipline (and the need to recruit students). Alcidamas' immediate concern, like that of his rivals, was to prepare his paying students for speaking in the Greek courts or in political assemblies or in public meetings; however, behind this there are real, if not always very profound, perceptions about speaking and writing as forms of human communication and their relative effectiveness in different situations.

1

τινες τῶν καλουμένων σοφιστῶν – although σοφιστής may at this period have a non-technical meaning – 'wise man' – here it clearly refers to the professional teacher. For the use of the word, see G.B. Kerferd, *The Sophistic Movement* (Cambridge,1981), 24 – 41. The speedy development of rhetoric in the last quarter of the fifth century BC led to sharp rivalry among the prominent practitioners and evidently to the emergence of some charlatans. The competitive atmosphere is well seen in Isoc.13.1–8, and Plato was by no means aloof from it – see G.J. De Vries, *A Commentary on the Phaedrus of Plato* (Amsterdam,1969), 15–18. For the jibe that some claimed knowledge of the whole of the art of rhetoric which they only knew in part, cf.Plato, *Phaedrus* 269b – c. This opening sentence is unlikely to be a veiled hit at Isocrates: it would be neither appropriate nor effective to say that he took no trouble over ἱστορία and παιδεία.

ἀπείρως ἔχουσι – key words: Alcidamas' stance throughout is that of the practical teacher rather than the theoriser, cf.§15.

διὰ βιβλίων – with no implication as to their form, e.g. papyrus rolls or tablets, cf. *IG* 2² 1.61 – τὸ βιβλίον τοῦ ψηφίσματος...'the text of the decree'. Reiske's conjecture διὰ βιβλίων is more appropriate than the MSS δι' ἀβεβαίων. It is possible to account for the mistake either as phonetic confusion or in visual terms: ΒΙΒΛΙΩΝ/ΒΕΒΑΙΩΝ in uncials. As MacDowell points out, the mistake is one of a type to which the scribe of X was particularly prone.

πολλοστὸν μέρος – the phrase is probably akin to expressions of numerical proportion: the part is one of very many, cf.τρίτον μέρος etc. See C. Carey ed., *Lysias:Selected Speeches* (Cambridge,1989), 167. This slightly unusual expression is one of several which suggest a relationship between *OWS* and Isoc.13, *Against the Sophists*. The crucial passages are: *OWS* §1–2, 15 ; Isoc.13.9, 11, 13, 30; 4.11ff. That some relationship exists can hardly be doubted, for the coincidences of vocabulary and phraseology are more than accidental. It is much less clear whether Alcidamas is 'replying' to Isocrates, or *vice versa*, or indeed whether both have a third party in their sights. There is no question of one treatise being a full-scale answer to the other (in spite of the similarity between Isoc. title and the alternative title – ΠΕΡΙ ΤΩΝ ΣΟΦΙΣΤΩΝ – of Alcidamas' work); it is more a matter of none-too-friendly point-scoring with deliberate echoes of wording. The evidence has been much discussed and all three views described above have been argued. I incline to think that it is Alcidamas who is criticising Isocrates in fairly general terms but no firm conclusion is possible. See O'Sullivan, 23 –31; G. Walberer, *Isokrates und Alkidamas* Diss. Hamburg, 1938; Milne, 21 –54 (a useful conspectus of discussions to the date of writing).

ἐπιχειρήσω κατηγορίαν ποιήσασθαι – the phraseology of the court-room comes naturally to Alcidamas; it should not be taken as evidence that the treatise was intended as a formal 'speech'.

2

οὐχ ὡς ἀλλοτρίαν – Alcidamas is keen to point out here and elsewhere (§7 and 30) that he is quite cognizant of a writer's skills; he simply wishes to put them in their place. The sentence in which he makes his point is, however, stylistically very clumsy: the three participle phrases unbalance it very awkwardly.

τὴν δύναμιν – Alcidamas is particularly fond of δύναμις to express 'capacity for', 'ability', or 'competence in' cf. §6, 9, 10, 29, 30, 33; No. 6, p.33.

τὸν βίον καταναλίσκοντας – Avezzù, 75 regards this as a probable reference to Isocrates and the length of time he took to compose e.g. the *Panegyrikos*. Isocrates is doubtless included but the reference is surely more general.

καὶ φιλοσοφίας – it is hard to give a precise meaning for φιλοσοφία at this period. It seems to denote both the methodical treatment of a subject (Isoc. 10.6; 4.10), and the human activity involved in pursuing it (which, being intellectual, might prejudice strength of character e.g. φιλοσοφοῦμεν ἄνευ μαλακίας – Thuc. ii.40). Alcidamas probably meant no more than a good background knowledge allied to the capacity to use it for practical purposes – not so far from Isocrates' usage.For a very full treatment of Isocrates' use of the word, see Wersdörfer, *passim*. For the contrast between Isocrates' and Plato's notions of φιλοσοφία and the prickly relationship between the two men, see J.S. Morrison, 'The Origins of Plato's Philosopher-Statesman', *CQ* n.s.viii (1958), 216–18; G.J. De Vries, *op.cit.*, 15–18.

ποιητὰς ἢ σοφιστὰς – the contrast is at first sight odd. The word ποιητής is regularly used simply to mean 'producer' or 'maker' and there need be no implication of poetry. Isocrates, for instance, criticises teachers who think that the art of teaching people to speak is like the τέχνη of a ποιητικοῦ πράγματος – 13.12. Here ποιητής is for Alcidamas clearly a term of criticism or limitation as against σοφιστής (cf. §34 where ῥήτωρ δεινός is plainly regarded as superior to the ποιητὴς λόγων), and there does indeed seem to be a general distinction of status between the 'script-writer' (ποιητής) who is like a craftsman and merely provides the words for a speech and the 'performer' (ἀγωνιστής) who may or may not provide the words but is the person who actually delivers in public – Isoc. 13.15; 15.92; Plato, *Euthyd.* 289d; *Phaedr.* 278e. Script-writers however had their *amour-propre* and Prodicus claimed for them that they inhabited the borderlands between philosophy and politics – Plato, *Euthyd.* 305b-c.

3

εὐεπίθετον – the meaning of the adjective is normally 'easy to attack' e.g. ἡμῖν ἂν εὐεπίθετος εἴη Thuc. vi.34.4, and this meaning would not be impossible here. However, ἐπίθετος can mean 'added', and 'easily added (to oneself)' i.e. 'easily acquired' fits better with the argument and the other two expressions in the sentence.

τῶν ἐνθυμημάτων καὶ τῶν ὀνομάτων – a language expression was often thought of as having two constituents: the words (ὀνόματα) and the ideas they expressed (ῥήματα or ἐνθυμήματα) – Plato, *Apol.* 17c ....λόγους....ῥήμασί τε καὶ ὀνόμασιν οὐδὲ κοσμημένους, cf. Isoc. 9.10; Plato, *Symp.* 198b, 199b, 221e. ἐνθύμημα is used by Alcidamas simply to mean a notion or argument, the normal meaning in pre-Aristotelian writers e.g. Aeschin. 2.110; Soph., *OC* 292, 1199; Isoc. 13.17. Later Aristotle used the word as a technical term – *enthymeme* – for a looser type of syllogism in which an often general or probable major premise produced a probable but not certain conclusion. See Kennedy, 97; M.F. Burnyeat, 'Enthymeme: Aristotle on the Rationality of Rhetoric' in A.O. Rorty ed., *Essays on Aristotle's* Rhetoric (Berkeley, Los Angeles, London, 1996), 88–115. ὄνομα is the regular Greek for 'word' (it was even applied to verbs – Aeschin. 3.72); ἔπος kept the notion of something spoken rather than the visible words of a text, cf. Aesch. *Suppl.* 179 τἄμ᾽ ἔπη δελτουμένας.

εὐπορία – one of Alcidamas' watchwords and one of the chief advantages he promises his students cf. §13, 19, 24, 34. It is a constant theme too in the *Rhetorica ad Alexandrum* ; each section of that work concludes with a similar formula: 'if we do this, εὐπορήσομεν' - e.g.1422a, 1423a etc.

τῷ καιρῷ – the concept of the καιρός crops up regularly in Greek thought from Hesiod onwards (it is post-Homeric). It occurs in many gnomic and proverbial sayings, e.g. Chilon – DK 88 B7; Hesiod,*WD*, 692; Democritus – DK 68 B94. Protagoras and Gorgias both seem to have tried to give the word a semi-technical definition for the purposes of rhetoric – Diog. Laert.ix.52; Dion. Hal. *De comp. verb.* 12. Thereafter, it is an accepted term of rhetorical vocabulary, becoming an important part of Isocrates' doctrine – see Wersdörfer, 55–72, and it is an important concept for Demosthenes too. See W. Schmid and O. Stählin, *Geschichte der griechischen Literatur* (München,1940), i.3.65; Kennedy, 66–7; Avezzù, 76–7; O'Sullivan, 91–4.

ταῖς ἐπιθυμίαις....εὐστόχως ἀκολουθῆσαι – the handling of audience reaction is developed in §22-23. The metaphor is from aiming a weapon; the extempore speaker, being sensitive to the mood of the audience, homes in on the target. See Avezzù, 75.

τὸν προσήκοντα λόγον εἰπεῖν – probably a reference to one of the features of self-conscious style which Gorgias also taught – τὸ πρέπον, 'what is fitting'. This was a major influence on Isocrates and it became one of the four classic virtues of style in the developed system of rhetoric from Theophrastus onwards. See Kennedy, 273–6; Wersdörfer, 18–31; M. Pohlenz, 'τὸ πρέπον: ein Beitrag zur Geschichte des griechischen Geistes', *Nachrichten der königlichen Gesellschaft der Wissenschaften zu Göttingen* (Phil–hist. Klasse), 1933.

4

ἐν πολλῷ δὲ χρόνῳ γράψαι.... – the three reasons which Alcidamas gives do not seem to make writing obviously easier than extempore speaking. They probably represent a deliberately crude version of how his chief rivals, Isocrates and his followers, went about their business.

παραθέμενον – agreeing with a suppressed τινά, the subject of all the infinitives. The sentence is awkwardly constructed as if all the infinitives were articular and form a neuter subject to which ῥᾴδιον refers. Such an extended list is unusual – see Kühner-Gerth[4] ii.3.

τῶν προγεγονότων σοφιστῶν – σοφιστής is here plainly used in the general, non-technical sense – 'wise man'.

5 – 8

What is worthwhile is obtained by hard work; what is easier is worth less. Moreover, if someone can cope with harder things, they can, with a little adjustment, manage easier things in the same category. So, good speakers can, with a little trouble, write good scripts; good script-writers, however, are not by virtue of their skill necessarily good speakers. Analogies from weight-lifting, javelin-throwing and archery reinforce the message.

The analogies are rather obvious and one of them would have been enough; the logic is elementary and directed at an ordinary rather than an intellectual audience, the illustrations being chosen from some of the normal recreations practised by younger people in the gymnasium.

5

ἔστι δ' ἄπαντα.... – the idea that good things are hard work and difficult to come by and that their opposites are easy is proverbial – Democritus DK B 182 τὰ μὲν καλὰ χρήματα τοῖς πόνοις ἡ μάθησις ἐξεργάζεται, τὰ δὲ αἰσχρὰ ἄνευ πόνων αὐτόματα καρποῦται; [Plut.] *De lib. educ.* 6C quotes as a proverb χαλεπὰ τὰ καλά. Cf. Hesiod, *WD* 289-92; Theognis 1025ff.; Epicharm. DK B 36; Soph. *El.* 945.

τὰ δὲ ταπεινὰ – ταπεινός refers to position – 'low-lying'. It can figuratively have a range of meanings from the pejorative (as here) to the approving ('humble'), or simply descriptive ('brought low', 'low in spirit'). See LSJ.

ἑτοιμότερον....ἐστιν – for this sense of 'more readily available', cf. Thuc. i.20.

6

λογογραφήσουσι – a nice double meaning with doubtless a slight sneer at the profession – 'will write scripts for speeches appropriately' or 'will be quite good logographers'.

ἠσκημένοις....γεγυμνασμένοις – the athletic metaphors link neatly to the examples which follow. They also reinforce the idea that training is as necessary for the orator as for the athlete.

ἀντίτυπος καὶ προσάντης – ἀντίτυπος may be a metaphor from coinage – 'the other side of the coin'. Hesychius (Latte) gives a range of meanings of which ἐναντιός is the most appropriate. For Alcidamas' acquaintance with the technicalities of coinage, cf. *Odysseus* §26.

7

ὁ μὲν γὰρ ἆραι μέγα φορτίον – the references here are to athletic training, not competition; there were no contests for weight-lifting in formal athletic games. There is, however, some evidence that weights were a part of training regimes – H.A.Harris, *Sport in Greece and Rome* (London,1972), 142-50. In choosing athletic analogies Alcidamas is obviously appealing to the typical interests of the young men who would be his most likely pupils.

διικνούμενος – for this sense of 'coming at' or 'reaching', cf. Thuc. vii.79.

τοῖς θάσσοσιν ὁμοδραμεῖν – 'to keep pace with', i.e. in training runs rather than in a race. ὁμοδραμέω is only found here; the sense is clear.

δυνάμενος ἐπισκόπως ἀκοντίζειν ἢ τοξεύειν – javelin-throwing in competition was normally a matter of competitive distance; in training, however, target practice was quite normal. The arguments in Antiphon's second *Tetralogy* turn on a boy accidentally killed because he got in the way of the javelin target (σκοπός) – *Tetr.* 2.2.4; 2.2.7; 2.3.6; 2.4.5. Archery was part of military and (later) ephebic training and there were local competitions, but it did not feature in the Great Games. See E.N. Gardiner, *Athletics of the Ancient World* (Oxford,1930), 27.

8

οὐκ ἄδηλον ..... οὐκ ἀφανὲς – the parallelism of the double negatives is clearly conscious 'style'. Alcidamas is rather annoyingly fond in this treatise of such negatived or double-negatived adjectives and adverbs, cf. §15, 20, 28, 34.

διαφέρων ἔσται λογοποιός – for the use of λογοποιός as 'speech-writer', see Plato, *Euthyd.* 289d where the skills of writing speeches and delivering them are also distinguished. Plato/Kleinias agrees with Alcidamas that those who compose cannot necessarily speak.

9 - 11

For politicians or pleaders in the courts or for those who address private meetings, speaking as the occasion requires is a necessity. Unexpected events and opportunities occur in which the tongue-tied seem laughable but those who can speak receive adulation. Emergencies need swift action, but script-writing needs time. What sensible person would want a skill which misses so many chances ? In a real-time situation in the courts or in politics a speaker would look ridiculous if he had to resort to his writing-tablet. Speakers cannot compel attention.

There are two main points in this section. The first is the obvious one that some public occasions absolutely require an on-the-spot response, and that the person who can only think in terms of what has been carefully prepared beforehand is at a great disadvantage. The second is to emphasize the width of that gap between 'speech-acts' and a composed text which ancient writing technology and script-habits necessarily imposed. A written text was much less helpful to an ancient speaker than it is to a modern one.

9

λέγειν μὲν ἐκ τοῦ παραυτίκα.... – Alcidamas links the essential skill which he is promoting to the three main interest-groups who would form the potential customers for any Greek teacher of rhetoric: political speakers, those who had to speak in the courts, and those who addressed private gatherings. The grouping is commonplace though the law usually comes first – Plato, *Phaedr.* 261a; *Soph.* 222c. Isocrates predictably has little time for the use of oratory in private affairs – 15. 227-8; 276. The present argument applies more to political debate. In the absence of cross-examination in the Greek courts, a ready wit and fluent response would have been needed much more in the *Boule* and the Assembly. However, Alcidamas points out justly that an unexpected turn in a prosecution speech may need a swift reaction too. ἰσόθεον τὴν γνώμην ἔχοντας – the exaggeration already reflects the 'star' potential of good speakers (or the high opinions rhetors had of themselves).

10

ὅταν γὰρ νουθετῆσαι.... – rhetoric is envisioned in an almost therapeutic role. Plato made such claims the subject of wicked irony, e.g. *Phaedr*. 289e where the speaker is said to charm juries and assemblies in the same way as enchanters charm vipers, spiders, scorpions and other wild things.

θυμουμένους – Vahlen's conjecture following Reiske is only one of many suggested to remedy the MS text; it gives the best sense. See Avezzù, 12.

τοὺς χρόνους τῶν καιρῶν – 'the time [needed to make use] of the opportunities'.

τίς ἂν φρονῶν ..... – the appeal to the sane, ordinary man was a commonplace, cf. §6; Isoc. 13.14; 10.10.

11

τίς ἀγορεύειν βούλεται τῶν πολιτῶν; – not quite the usual wording. The exact formula by which the κῆρυξ invited the start of discussion in the Assembly seems to have varied a little. The normal wording in the late fifth century BC and onwards was τίς ἀγορεύειν βούλεται; – Aristoph. *Ach*. 45; *Thesm*. 379; *Ekkles*. 130; Dem. *De cor*. 170. According to Aeschines 1.23, however, the older, more correct formula uttered first (whose passing he laments in 3. 2-4) was τίς ἀγορεύειν βούλεται τῶν ὑπὲρ πεντήκοντα ἔτη γεγονότων. It seems likely that the shortened version or something like it was standard and that the custom of allowing the over-50s to speak before anyone else fell into disuse. See M.H. Hansen, *The Athenian Ecclesia* (Copenhagen,1989), ii.98 n.15.

τοῦ ὕδατος....ἤδη ῥέοντος – the water-clock, consisting of an open upper vessel with a hole just above the base and a lower container into which the water flowed, rationed the time for speakers in the courts. The time allowed depended on the seriousness of the case and was measured in terms of 'fills' (χόες) of the upper vessel. A late fifth century BC example from the Athenian Agora held two χόες and had a six minute running time – S. Young, *Hesperia* viii (1939), 274-84. Permitted speech times probably varied from 30 minutes to about 18 minutes for lead speakers, and from 10 minutes to 6 minutes for second speakers (reading time for laws and witness statements did not count). See P.J. Rhodes, *A Commentary on the Aristotelian* Athenaion Politeia (Oxford,1981), 719-21.

ἐπὶ τὸ γραμματεῖον – ridiculous it would indeed seem to be, for γραμματεῖον usually signified either a waxed or whitened wood tablet. For a speaker touched with nerves, a text without word-division or punctuation, written quite small, would be exceedingly hard to read.

εἰ μὲν ἤμεν τύραννοι – tyrants can compel and choose their timing; the speaker in the Athenian courts or Athenian politics has to speak to a timetable set in advance by others. Avezzù, 77 sees a deeper political significance in this passage, regarding the water-clock and the herald's summons as symbols of ἰσηγορία and Athenian freedom of speech, and comparing Theseus' famous defence of equality before the published laws in Eur. *Suppl.* 428ff.; the γραμματεῖον on the other hand implies 'tempi e modalità esclusivi'. The passage certainly shows an appreciation of the open society and the role of open debate and hints at the potentiality of the written word for political control, but it is probably a mistake to read too much into it beyond that.

ἐπὶ τὴν ἀκρόασιν – it is assumed that, even if official written texts are produced, they will be disseminated largely by word of mouth. See W.V. Harris, *Ancient Literacy* (Cambridge, Mass. and London,1991), 50-1.

† ἐναντίως ἔχουσιν ἀκριβῶς † < .... > – the text has gone beyond recall here nor is the likely sequence of thought at all clear.

12 – 13

If speeches are carefully scripted in detail, losing any sense of spontaneity or reality, and through their artificiality alienate the audience, *<they will have the opposite effect to what is intended >*. The proof of this is that speech-writers for the courts make efforts to avoid the impression of contrived language and imitate the style of extempore speakers; the closer they come to natural, spoken language, the more successful their speeches. Should not training for speakers learn this lesson ?

Alcidamas here points to the paradox of the successful speech-writer's art: what is composed must be capable of being delivered as if it were natural 'ear-language' rather than artificial 'eye-language'. He therefore argues that rhetorical training should go for the real thing rather than the illusion of it which logographers cultivate.

12

τοῖς ὀνόμασιν ἐξειργασμένοι.... – i.e. the texts are completed compositions with exact wording; they are not acts of communication in which one person speaks to another (λόγοις).

ἀληθείαις – the plural is not found before the fourth century BC. Cf. Isoc. 9.5; 15.283; *Odysseus* §13.

ἐμπιμπλᾶσι < .... > – there is clearly a lacuna for the conditional lacks an apodosis. The general sense required is clear – 'they will not be effective'.

τὰς ἀκριβείας – Alcidamas uses the plural (cf.§25) to indicate a particularly precise and artful <u>style</u> in which the wording is carefully chosen and carefully arranged. This is very similar to Isocrates' usage; see Wersdörfer, 138. ἀκρίβεια and ἀκριβῶς on the other hand tend simply to designate the form of a set, written text. There is more than the hint of an adverse value-judgement though: ἀκρίβεια and ἀκριβείαι often have a pernickety sense – Plato, *Gorgias* 487c; Isoc. 7.40. See also K.J. Dover, *Lysias and the* Corpus Lysiacum (Berkeley and Los Angeles,1968), 155; O'Sullivan, 43–5. For a more wide-ranging examination of this concept, see D. Kurz, *AKPIBEIA: Das Ideal der Exaktheit bei den Griechen bis Aristoteles* (Göppingen,1970).

14 – 15

Written texts can cause anomalies in life-style, for texts cannot cover all eventualities and some extempore utterance is inevitable; two different styles of language are therefore produced which can be remarkably incongruous and leave an author liable to uncomfortable criticism. It is a poor look-out if a person who claims to be a philosopher or to teach others is so dependent on books or texts that, without them, he appears as ignorant as the uneducated, and is lost for words unless he has time to ponder, and can teach the theory but lacks the practice.

The first point hints at the interesting notion that language-style may be a symptom, or even a cause, of life-style. The proposition that modes of language composition (especially writing) seriously influence the way we think has been much argued in recent years in the context of debates about literacy and orality. Incongruities between carefully composed and extempore language must have seemed the more obvious to someone well acquainted with the relentless stylistic patterning which seems to have been one of Gorgias' methods of teaching. This section also connects with another practice of the sophists (and doubtless of their teaching too): extempore display oratory was one of Gorgias' regular 'turns' at his public appearances. However, a more serious point is indicated, namely, that knowledge or competence which has not been internalized has a very limited usefulness.

14

ἀποδοκιμάζειν – the verb is frequently used generally to mean 'reject', but the sense of 'reject after examination' is usually present. See LSJ.

βίον....ἀνώμαλον – the geographical idea of unevenness and not being on the level leads to the notions of inconsistency and not fitting in to a pattern. People did not know whether to think well or badly of Alcibiades διὰ τὴν τῆς φύσεως ἀνωμαλίαν – Plut. *Alcib.* 16.

γεγραμμένους ἐπίστασθαι λόγους – the infinitive phrase forms the subject of πέφυκεν and is used as if it were articular, cf. §4.

τυποῖ – the verb from τύπος is not common and always has the sense of stamping an impression, even when used figuratively, cf. Gorgias, *Hel.* 13. The emphasis here is not on the mere process of drafting but on the fact that writing, once formed, is hard to change, like a stamped pattern; this may be a metaphor from coin manufacture.

τὰ μὲν ὑποκρίσει....καὶ φαῦλα – a clear indication that the 'separation of styles' was already commonly acknowledged in intellectual circles; the language register appropriate to drama and poetry is assumed to be on a higher plane than that of every-day discourse. For a good account of the early development of this awareness, see O'Sullivan, 6-22. Alcidamas is quite prepared to admit that extempore speeches may make a less polished impression than scripted ones – §31. For the different styles required for delivery and for reading, cf. Aristot. *Rhet.* iii.1413b-1414a.

15

{ἀντιλέγειν} – the MSS ἀντιλέγειν makes no sense and Vahlen was probably right to exclude it. Radermacher's ἄν τι λέγειν is ingenious but involves the insertion of < περὶ > before φιλοσοφίας.

εὐθέως δὲ περὶ τοῦ προτεθέντος – probably a reference to one of the well-known moments in Gorgias' public appearances – the invitation to the audience to suggest a topic (προβάλλετε) on which he would then deliver an extempore speech (Philostrat. *Vit.Soph.* 482). It is highly likely that he trained his pupils in this skill: hence Alcidamas' contempt for those who cannot speak extempore on themes proposed to them.

λόγων μὲν τέχνας – Alcidamas must be referring to writing about speech-making rather than using τέχνη in the sense of a specimen speech (a meaning sometimes suggested): the contrast is between theory and practice, and λόγων is meaningless if τέχνας already means 'speeches'.

καὶ γὰρ..... – introduces the final explanatory sentence. Isocrates too was fond of concluding absurdities in similar style. See J.D. Denniston, rev. K.J. Dover, *The Greek Particles* 2nd ed. (Oxford,1966), 108-9.

16 – 17

A person who is used to paying great attention to the exact vocabulary and construction of a text will necessarily, on turning to extempore speech, find that his mind cannot cope, and will panic and become bad-tempered about everything since he is doing the opposite of what he is used to. He will be like those with speech-impediments and will never speak readily and genially. Just as prisoners who have been released do not move naturally but continue to use their limbs in the ways their chains required, so writing produces slowness in the mind and sets a blockage to fluency.

In emphasizing that quickness of wit and reaction are needed for extempore speaking and that the composition of scripts involves different, slower processes of mind, Alcidamas is only saying what would readily be recognized by many court-room lawyers and politicians today. The analogy he uses was vivid enough to be remembered by later writers and it is possible that it originates from Socrates, who seems to have been fond of striking analogies when talking of the limitations of the written word.

16

μετ 'ἀκριβείας καὶ ῥυθμοῦ – very probably a reference to that artificially balanced style which is such a feature of Gorgias' extant works and with which his pupils doubtless became very familiar.

τὰ ῥήματα συντιθέναι – ῥῆμα (which is often contrasted with ὄνομα cf. §2) indicates a unit of predication – it 'says something', which may be one word or a phrase or several lines. See Plato, *Crat.* 399b; Aeschin. 3.72; K.J. Dover ed. *Aristophanes* Frogs (Oxford,1993), 202-3.

τῇ τῆς διανοίας κινήσει – normally thought is reckoned to be very speedy, e.g. the simile in Homer, *Iliad* xv.80–3; the pseudo-Aristotelian treatise *De lineis insecabilibus* describes ἡ διανοίας κίνησις as the swiftest thing there is – 968a25.

ἀπορίας καὶ θορύβου – for the same diagnosis, cf. §8.

τῶν ἰσχνοφώνων – can mean either 'weak-voiced' or 'with a speech-impediment'. This may be a sideswipe at Isocrates who took to teaching because he had neither the voice for a professional career as an orator nor the self-confidence (τόλμα) – Isoc. 12. 9-11; 5. 81; *Letter* 8.7.

ὑγρῶς – the basic notion of wetness and dampness passes over to the idea of flexibility, even to human physical suppleness – Plato, *Theaet.* 162b, or divine smoothness – *Symp.* 196a.

17

ἀλλ 'ὥσπερ οἱ διὰ μακρῶν χρόνων ἐκ δεσμῶν.... – the difficulty of escaping from habits of written composition is vividly illustrated. It is important to note that Alcidamas is not referring simply to what we would call 'style' but to different ways of generating language: written composition and improvisation demand different mind-sets. There may be some connection between this apt and striking analogy and Plato's famous allegory of the Cave in *Republic* 514a-517a. Both analogies involve prisoners released from a long period of bondage who are unable at first to escape from the habits formed when they were tied up (habits of perception and interpretation in Plato, habits of movement and composition in Alcidamas).The applications and development of the stories are admittedly on different planes, but there are similarities, and, in view of Alcidamas' evident acquaintance with Platonic/Socratic ideas (see §27-8), it is perhaps noteworthy that it is the <u>soul</u> (ψυχή) which is affected by the restrictions imposed by writing habits.

Alcidamas' analogy made an impression on the author of [Plut.] *De lib. educ.* 6F. He used a clearly recognizable version of Alcidamas' image to warn students against becoming too set in their speaking habits so that they could not improvise when occasion demanded.

τὴν ἄσκησιν ἄπορον.... – there is possibly an echo here of the ideas explored in Plato, *Phaedr.* 271a-c where speaking and writing are also distinguished.

εὐροίας ἀπάσης – a regular rhetorical word for a flow of words; Philostratus uses it of Favorinus, a minor sophist, who was said to be a fluent improviser – *Vit. Soph.* 491; Plato, *Phaedr.* 238c.

18 – 21

Written texts are hard to grasp and remember (as well as embarrassing to forget). Improvisation only requires you to learn the basic arguments leaving the actual words to be supplied on the spot. The individual words of a text are very numerous, the basic arguments relatively few and important. Moreover, if an improviser forgets an argument, he will be flexible enough to pass on and return to it in a suitable place when he remembers, and there will be no embarrassment. If someone who relies on a written text, however, omits something in the heat of the moment, there will be panic, digression, drying-up and long pauses, and his collapse will be unseemly, ridiculous and hard to remedy.

These sections which are concerned with the advantages of remembering a series of headings or main ideas as against the word-for-word memorization of whole texts present sensible and straightforward arguments; there are no tricks or academic systems.

18

τὴν μάθησιν....καὶ τὴν μνήμην – there is a not entirely consistent distinction between grasping/understanding a text (μάθησις) and committing it to memory (μνήμη). Although it is sometimes said that the beginnings of formal memory-techniques (which associated things to be remembered with visual order – the so-called 'places' and 'pictures') went back to Simonides and Hippias (with his legendary memory stunts), there is no trace of them until later. Aeschylus and Sophocles talk of memory in terms of waxed writing tablets in the mind (Aesch. *Prom.* 789; *Suppl.* 179; *Choeph.* 450; *Eum.* 275; Soph. *Trach.* 683; *Philoct.* 1325). Plato thinks of writing and pictures in the mind (*Phileb.* 38e-39b), and in *Theaetet.* 191c-d he has the more intriguing model of blocks of wax (of varying size and quality depending on the individual) which receive impressions as from a signet ring. Euenos of Paros is said to have put some of his 'indirect censures' (παραψόγους) into rhythmic form to aid the memory (Plato, *Phaedr.* 267a), but apart from this there are no descriptions of techniques nor is there a section on memory in the *Rhetorica ad Alexandrum*. It is probable that the beginnings of systematic memory-technique were introduced to rhetoric by Theodectes. See H. Blum, *Die antike Mnemotechnik* (Hildesheim,1969), 41-55, 87-92.

ἐν τοῖς ἀγῶσι - not necessarily referring just to law-suits but to any situations in which adversaries meet. See LSJ.

τοὺς αὐτοσχεδιασμούς – αὐτοσχεδιασμός may be Alcidamas' own coinage since the word is not found elsewhere – a natural enough formation from αὐτοσχεδιάζω.

δηλοῦν – a slightly unusual absolute use of which Alcidamas is quite fond – §19, 20, 24, 33. Cf. Lysias 10.7 περὶ ἑνὸς εἰπών, περὶ πάντων ἐδηλώσεν.

καὶ τῶν ἐνθυμημάτων – Avezzù following Blass would delete this phrase which is found after τῶν ὀνομάτων in the MSS. I prefer Sauppe's solution, followed by MacDowell, of transposing it.

19

τοῖς δ᾽ὀνόμασι πολλάκις τοῖς αὐτοῖς – perhaps referring to

the likelihood of coincidences of wording and their dangers for the memorizer rather than the trite fact that there are many common words.

δυσανάληπτος – occurs only here in this sense.

20

ἄδηλον τὴν αἰσχύνην ἔχουσιν – the focus now shifts: the audience need not be aware of memory lapses in extempore speeches.

συνεξεσμένων – perf. partcp. pass. of συγξέω. Smoothness and polish are the hallmarks of the prepared written text.

οὐ χαλεπὸν ὑπερβῆναι ..... – a very awkward construction since, if the text is sound, ἁψάμενον must go with λόγον; it would be more natural for the orator to fasten on the next arguments rather than the speech. It may simply be that the sentence slips from dative + infinitive to accusative + infinitive, but the awkwardness remains.

21

τοῖς δὲ γεγραμμένα λέγουσιν – i.e. those who have memorized a written text word-for-word and are delivering it.

ὑπὸ τῆς ἀγωνίας – ἀγωνία and ἀγωνιάω can have the sense both of a contest and the tension and pain that goes with it – Dem. 18.33; Plato, *Protag.* 333e.

καὶ μακροὺς μὲν χρόνους ἐπίσχειν – Alcidamas' diagnosis obviously comes from experience: a sense of an embarrassing situation, amusement, and a feeling of wanting to help are often part of an audience's reaction to the long pauses and confusion of a speaker who loses his way in a prepared text.

δυσεπικούρητον – LSJ gives 'hard to meet', but the meaning here plainly derives from ἐπικουρέω; the audience does indeed find it hard to come to the rescue.

22 – 23

Improvisers make better use of an audience's reaction than text-users who often miss their opportunities by working things out too carefully in advance. Text-users sometimes speak too much for an audience's taste, sometimes too little. Audience response cannot easily be foreseen and improvisers can make adjustments as the occasion demands.

Alcidamas concentrates first on the length of speeches, but these two sections introduce a more general point about oratory and audience reaction which he will develop later. The really successful orator has a living relationship with the audience, and, if not shackled by a pre-determined text, can sense this, develop it and exploit it.

22

τὰ συγγράμματα – i.e. their finished texts. The word usually implies a completed document in a literary or a legal context. See LSJ.

23

ταμιεύεσθαι τοὺς λόγους – a similar metaphor occurs in one of the phrases Aristotle quotes from Alcidamas: [the orator? is] ....οἰκονόμος τῶν ἀκουόντων ἡδονῆς 'the steward of the audience's pleasure'. See p.35 no.20.

πρὸς τὰς δυνάμεις τῶν γνωμῶν – Avezzù's text following Bekker/Sauppe gives better sense than the awkward τῶν λόγων preferred by Radermacher. δύναμις is here applied to an abstraction (γνωμῶν); Alcidamas more often uses it to indicate a human capacity for something.

καὶ τὰ μήκη συντέμνειν....διὰ μακροτέρων δηλοῦν – the skill of expanding subject-matter (μακρολογία or αὔξησις) or compressing it (βραχυλογία or ταπείνωσις) was evidently a stock-in-trade of teachers of rhetoric from early days. With heavy irony Tisias and Gorgias are credited by Plato with the discovery of συντομίαν τε λόγων καὶ ἄπειρα μήκη περὶ πάντων – ' both the abbreviation of topics and interminable length on every subject'. Protagoras was said to teach the same skills and to be a master of them. Plato, *Phaedr.* 267a-b; *Protag.* 334e,335b; Aristot., *Rhet.* iii.1418a36. The techniques are taken for granted in *Rhet. ad Alex.* 6.

24 – 26

Extempore speakers can also make better use of ideas which they pick up from their adversaries or which occur to them on the spot; they can expand as necessary without distorting their speeches. Those who have composed carefully in advance, however, either cannot use extra material or, if they do, risk upsetting the balance of the text and, by a mixture of improvisation with careful composition, produce confusion and lack of harmony. Who would want such a skill which cannot make use of present or chance advantage ?

Alcidamas extends the idea that the situation in a law-court or in debate is a 'live' one which throws up opportunities; he also points to the fact that arguments and expressions may well occur spontaneously to someone who is stimulated and at full stretch. In both cases the extempore speaker can use the advantage whilst the text-user is hampered.

24

τὴν συντονίαν τῆς διανοίας – the metaphor is musical but not to do with harmony; σύντονος is used of the strings of musical instruments meaning 'taut' or 'stretched', the meaning thence being transferred to feelings or actions or states of mind. See LSJ σύντονος. The notion here is that the skilled impromptu speaker is necessarily on his toes with a keenly alert mind.

ἐν τάξει – probably 'structure' in the sense of the disposition of the parts of a court-room speech. In Alcidamas' day the pattern was probably quite simple: prologue, narration, proofs, and epilogue (with evidence of distinction between types of proof and probability). See Theodectes *fr.* 133 (Rose); Plato, *Phaedr.* 266d-267d. For a cautious view of the early development of speech structures, see T. Cole, *The Origins of Rhetoric in Ancient Greece* (Baltimore,1991), 22-6.

πλείω τῶν ἐσκεμμένων – the passive use of the participle is unusual; the verb usually has an active meaning. See LSJ σκέπτομαι.

τὸν λόγον ἀνώμαλον – the registers of written and spoken language are incongruous and therefore produce a result which is uneven. The metaphors used to describe language style are varied and experimental for some time. Aristotle criticizes Alcidamas' style in terms of 'coldnesses'; he also talks of style as having 'mass' or 'bulk' – *Rhet.* iii.1407b. See

O'Sullivan, 7; K.J. Dover ed., *Aristophanes* Frogs (Oxford,1997), 14.

25

τοὺς αὐτοματισμούς – i.e. expressions that generate themselves in response to stimuli.

ἀλλ' ἀναγκαῖον [sc.] τινά – the change to the singular is clumsy.

συνερείπειν – only found here; the sense is obvious.

τὰ δ'εἰκῇ – εἰκῇ λέγειν was a common phrase in rhetorical language for extempore speaking cf. §29,33; Plato, *Apol.* 17c; Isoc. 4. 12.

διάφωνον – Sauppe's suggestion following Reiske supplies a more consistent sense than the MS ἄφωνον which Avezzù prefers.

26

τῶν ἄλλων τεχνῶν ἐπὶ τὸ βέλτιον – it is taken for granted that a τέχνη leads to human progress and improvement. For the importance and relative novelty of this idea, see E.R. Dodds, *The Ancient Concept of Progress* (Oxford,1973), 11ff.

εὐπορήμασιν – εὐπόρημα is not found elsewhere.

27 – 28

Written speeches should be thought of, not as the real thing, but as images and imitations of it. They are like statues and other artistic representations of real life which are attractive but fixed in their form and no use for actually getting things done. A speech which is given extempore is a living thing; a written speech is like an image which has no life in it.

There are unmistakeable resonances here with Plato. The idea that written speeches are 'images and models and imitations' of real speeches is uncannily akin to the Platonic 'theory' of Forms in which actual objects in the world have an essential relationship to a perfect original which is the true reality. This particularly recalls the allegory of the Cave in *Republic* 514aff. in which the objects seen by tethered prisoners are in fact only shadows thrown on a wall. However, the links here are less with the *Republic* than with the well-known passages in the *Phaedrus* in which the limitations of writing are discussed (264c; 275a-b; 275d). It is beyond reasonable doubt that there is a connection; the nature of it is disputable.

27

εἴδωλα καὶ σχήματα καὶ μιμήματα λόγων – the most obvious echo of Plato's ideas; it is hard to believe that Alcidamas had not come across some version of the theory of Forms and remembered it as apt for his purposes. For the difficulties and complexities of the Platonic theory of Forms, see J. Annas, *An Introduction to Plato's Republic* (Oxford,1981), 217-41, 252-66; C.J. Rowe, *Plato* (Brighton,1984), 52-82. It has been suggested that Plato may have been influenced by Alcidamas in the formation of his thinking with regard to both the theory of Forms and his ideas about literature in general. However, the connections between §28 and the *Phaedrus* strongly suggest that the influence was in the other direction. See N.J. Richardson, ' The Contest Of Homer and Hesiod and Alcidamas' *Mouseion*', *CQ* n.s. xxxi (1981), 1-10; G. Walberer, *Isokrates und Alkidamas* Diss. Hamburg, 1938, 39ff.; W. Steidle, 'Redekunst und Bildung bei Isokrates', *Hermes* 80 (1952), 287–92.

ἔχοιμεν – Avezzù prefers ἔχοιμι which seems logical, but in fact the odd personal opinion is often embedded in deliberately generalized comment e.g. §18 – νομίζω δὲ....πάντες γὰρ ἂν ὁμολογήσειαν....; §22-24 – ἡγοῦμαι δὲ καὶ....ὁμοίως ὁρῶμεν .....

τέρψιν μὲν....χρῆσιν δ' οὐδεμίαν.... – the contrast between the beauty of the image which is less useful and the usefulness of reality which is less beautiful is not really Platonic. Plato does admit that image-making can produce a κήλησις which gives an impression of reality – *Rep.* 601a-b.

28

ἐνὶ σχήματι – simply 'a single form' - not contrasted with reality as σχήματα above.

ἐπὶ τῶν καιρῶν ἀκίνητος ὤν – even Isocrates was prepared to admit the inflexibility of the text when he was off-guard (13.10-13).

εὐμορφίας – Dobree's conjecture is one of several which try to correct the MS εὐπορίας. It is an improvement on Radermacher's εὐπρεπείας and is clearly preferable to Gomperz's θεωρίας which Avezzù prints.

λόγος ἐμψυχός ἐστι καὶ ζῇ – Alcidamas, in thus vividly characterizing the difference between direct, person-to-person communication and communication recreated from a text, highlights a difficulty facing the Greek orator. He could be, and plainly was, criticized for simply reading a speech, particularly if the delivery was too contrived (*Rhet. ad Alex.* 1444a); what he needed was real, 'live' communication with the audience or the illusion of it, cf. §13.

The striking idea of speech as an animate, living thing is certainly related to Plato, *Phaedrus* 275d-276a. There Socrates tells the story of the god, Theuth, the proud inventor of writing, who brings his invention to Thamos, the king of Egyptian Thebes. Thamos then expresses considerable reservations about the benefits of writing and the illusions it will produce. In the amplification of the story which Socrates gives to Phaedrus he compares writing to painting (ζωγραφία): paintings give the illusion of life but, when questioned, they cannot answer back. So it is with writing: writing cannot answer back either. The clinching evidence for the connection between the *Phaedrus* and *OWS* comes with the answer Phaedrus gives to Socrates' subsequent suggestion of an alternative mode to writing 'which is written with knowledge in the soul of the one who has understanding' (ὃς μετ' ἐπιστήμης γράφεται ἐν τῇ τοῦ μανθάνοντος ψυχῇ). Phaedrus replies: 'You mean the living and animate speech of the knowledgeable man, of which writing could rightly be called a kind of image' (τὸν τοῦ εἰδότος λόγον λέγεις ζῶντα καὶ ἔμψυχον οὗ ὁ γεγραμμένος εἴδωλον ἄν τι λέγοιτο δικαίως). The coincidences of thought and vocabulary between this and Alcidamas' text cannot be accidental.

There are no close parallels. Plato elsewhere and Aristotle appear to make the same comparison using an identical phrase (ὥσπερ ζῷον) to refer respectively to a speech (λόγος) and plots (μῦθοι). However, these passages are concerned with the way in which the parts of a speech and a plot fit together and form a consistent whole – like the parts of the body – not with the character of spoken language. *Phaedr.* 264c; *Poetics* 1459a. The deadness of the graven image as a form of contrast was familiar enough, e.g. Aristoph. *Frogs* 537b-539a (Dover). Isocrates contrasts memorials in the form of images with those in words, preferring the latter for a civilized person, and he does twice call λόγος an εἴδωλον ψυχῆς – 9.73-5; 3.7.

The author of the pseudo-Demosthenic *Erotikos* 16 points to the failure of images to express the soul, but none of these comes near to the idea of spoken communication as alive and in contrast to an inanimate text.

Who influenced whom ? I think there can be little doubt that Alcidamas took his ideas and phraseology either from a reading of the *Phaedrus* or directly from Socrates himself (Plato may well not have shared Socrates' attitudes to writing).

Attempts to link this passage with a supposed reference to the politician Theramenes' rhetorical writing are strained and far-fetched – W. Süss, *RhM* 66(1911),183-9; *contra* K.J. Dover ed., *Aristophanes* Frogs (Oxford,1997), 146; Avezzù, 78.

ἐνεργείας – Reiske's emendation is surely right; the MSS εὐεργεσίας which Avezzù accepts involves a rather strained meaning with far less appropriate sense, and the change is easily accounted for. The essential idea is that written texts lack the presence of something which is alive; Aristotle defines ἐνεργεία in just this way in *Rhet.* iii.1411b-1412a.

29 – 30

It may seem paradoxical to criticize writing whilst making use of it to publicize a point of view and to gain a reputation, and to praise extempore speeches whilst still devoting time to methodical study, and to think chance more productive than forethought, and those who speak as instinct dictates more sensible than those who prepare texts. However, I do not rule out the capacity for writing; I think it inferior to improvisation. I am not using a text in order to boast, but to point out to arrogant writers that I can refute their arguments with little trouble.

These two chapters begin the conclusion and face the obvious paradox that the author is writing a text to criticize the writing of texts. His answer here is an amplification of what he said in §2 – that writing is a by-product (πάρεργον) of learning to speak. There is also an unashamed note of self-advertisement and self-justification which strongly suggests that the treatise was intended as a weapon in the 'marketing war' between rival teachers of rhetoric for which there is abundant evidence.

29

ἴσως ἄν οὖν εἴποι τις – the typical personalized objection (followed by answers) to head off possible criticism. It was almost a cliché, whether in court, public meetings or philosophical argument. Cf. Plato, *Crito* 48a11.

κατηγορεῖν μὲν τῆς γραφικῆς δυναμέως – κατηγορέω is more often used of persons, but there are parallels – Dem. 18.266; Isoc. 3.4.

τὰς ἀποδείξεις ποιούμενον – almost 'displaying advertisements'. ἀπόδειξις became a technical term in Aristotelian logic for the proof of a syllogism, but at this point it had no specialized meaning. Bekker's ἐπιδείξεις which Avezzù prefers makes the reference more precise ('display speeches') but is unnecessary.

παρὰ τοῖς ῞Ελλησιν – the first generation of sophists did a lot of travelling, sometimes with an entourage of pupils. Alcidamas and his contemporaries probably had to do the same; for, whilst the pupil-market for rhetoric had grown, so had the competition. See G.B. Kerferd, *The Sophistic Movement* (Cambridge,1981), 22-3.

περὶ φιλοσοφίαν – elsewhere, Alcidamas' use of φιλοσοφία seems close to Isocrates' usage – 'methodical study' (see §2). Here it may be that Alcidamas is referring generally to his technical writing about rhetoric in addition to the present treatise. There are grounds for thinking that he wrote a τέχνη, and some have thought that the *Mouseion* had connections with teaching rhetoric.

προυργιαίτερον – a curiously formed adjective from the contracted phrase προὔργου (= πρὸ ἔργου) 'suitable for the job'. There is no positive adjectival form but the phrase was useful enough to give birth to a comparative (a superlative προυργιαίτατος is attested by the *Suda* and Hesychius). Reiske suggested προυργιαίτεραν but there is no need for change.

30

τούτους εἴρηκα τοὺς λόγους – as if Alcidamas is speaking to the reader through his writing; it is not an indication that his treatise is a 'speech'.

τοῖς ἐπὶ ταύτῃ τῇ δυνάμει σεμνυνομένοις – probably Isocrates and his school; there was no love lost between rival rhetoricians.

ἀποκρύψαι καὶ καταλῦσαι – the sense is clear and ἀποκρύπτω must mean something like 'blot out'. However, the usage is unusual enough and unparalleled enough to raise questions. Reiske proposed κατακλῦσαι which makes the doublet more consistent but does not quite answer the difficulty. Did Alcidamas perhaps write ἀποκρούσαι ?

31 – 32

I use writing for the publication of my work. I advise those who hear me often in public to judge from that experience, but, for those who have not heard me for some time or who have never come across me, I offer some of my writings. If people are used to hearing speeches delivered from texts, they may underestimate my improvisations. It is also easier to observe intellectual progress through written speeches – not so easy in improvisation since it is hard for people to recall what they have heard. Writing speeches leaves a memorial and gratifies ambition.

Alcidamas acknowledges the drawbacks of impromptu speaking from a promotional point of view because of its ephemeral nature. He candidly admits that he wants to leave records of his achievements and gratify his self-esteem. Some modern scholars have been disapproving, but these attitudes were common to many of the sophists and indeed to Isocrates also.

31

τῶν ἐπιδείξεων εἵνεκα – Alcidamas is probably thinking not only of his show-pieces like the *Encomium of Nais* or the *Encomium of Proteus the dog* but of more technical pieces like the present work. ἐπιδείξις can be used of a demonstration in general as well as a formal, set speech.

εἰς τοὺς ὄχλους ἐκφερομένων – an interesting hint that rhetors may have used hand-outs or perhaps texts to buy at demonstrations (rather as recordings are often available after a celebrity musical recital today). For logographers' speeches as home reading and as models, see S. Usher, 'Lysias and his clients', *GRBS* 17 (1976), 37–9. For a survey of the early development of text circulation, see W.V. Harris, *Ancient Literacy* (Cambridge, Mass. and London,1991), 84-8.

παρακελευόμεθα – Alcidamas now moves consistently to the grander first person plural for his conclusion.

ὑπὲρ ἅπαντος τοῦ προτεθέντος – cf. §15.

διὰ χρόνου – χρόνος without an adjective signifies an unspecified (but substantial) period of time, cf. Xen. *Cyr.* 1.4.28.

ἐλάττονα τῆς ἀξίας δόξαν – the implication being that on any one particular occasion the improviser might not be on form; you could only judge on the basis of several hearings.

32

σημεῖα τῆς ἐπιδόσεως – the prospect of swift, orderly progress was central to the rhetor's and the sophist's claims: it is the first advantage that Protagoras offers when challenged by Socrates on behalf of the young Hippocrates. Hippocrates will ἑκάστης ἡμέρας ἀεὶ ἐπὶ τὸ βέλτιον ἐπιδιδόναι – Plato, *Protag.* 318a. Likewise the assertion of some sophists that learning rhetoric was like learning to read and write implied methodical progress towards an achieveable skill – Isoc. 13.10.

ὥσπερ ἐν κατόπτρῳ – looking at the evidence supplied by written texts is like seeing the progress of your soul in a mirror; so perhaps in Alcidamas' phrase about the *Odyssey* – καλὸν ἀνθρωπίνου βίου κάτοπτρον (p.37, no.25) – reading the *Odyssey* is like seeing a reflection of human life and gives the opportunity to study it.

τῇ φιλοτιμίᾳ χαριζόμενοι – a candid admission of an attitude shared by many of Alcidamas' contemporaries, however disagreeable to Anglo-Saxon modesty cf. Isoc. 4.3, 12-14; V. Buchheit, *Untersuchungen zur Theorie des Genos Epideiktikon von Gorgias bis Aristoteles* (München, 1960), 41-5.

33 – 34

I am not undervaluing writing in promoting improvisation. Speakers must be prepared in their use of ideas and structure but must leave the choice of words to the moment; the written text does not make good use of opportunity in the way that improvised wording does. If someone wants to be an orator rather than a script-writer, to use opportunities well rather speak to a text accurately, to have an audience's goodwill, to have flexibility and a good memory and to acquire really relevant speaking skills, would that person not naturally practise improvisation and be thought to be acting sensibly in making writing a by-product.

Alcidamas' conclusion seems to retreat a little from earlier positions: writing is now allowed to have more advantages than at the start, both because Alcidamas must justify his own position as someone who has composed epideictic speeches and because Alcidamas, the salesman, cannot afford to provoke too much offence by rubbishing an opposition which already had a considerable reputation. With hindsight this can be seen as something of a rear-guard action in the face of developments in literacy and rhetoric which were already becoming unstoppable.

33

οὐδ᾽ ὡς....ἀξιόν ἐστι πιστεύειν – not what was said at the start (§3ff.); the conclusion has to leave the impression of fair-minded, reasonable judgement, cf. Isoc. 13.21ff.

μετὰ προνοίας – the need for preparation has already been hinted at in §18–19: the extempore speaker has his ideas (ἐνθυμήματα) organized and memorized. However, perhaps in order not to give away the secrets of the course for which pupils will have to pay, Alcidamas gives surprisingly little information on what an extempore speaker actually needs to do in advance (indeed in §29 προνοία is used to refer to scripted speeches).

34

ῥήτωρ....δεινὸς ἀλλὰ μὴ ποιητὴς λόγων ἱκανός – i.e. what Alcidamas offers is on a different plane from simply writing adequate speeches, cf. §2. It has been suggested that ποιητὴς λόγων is an attempt to nettle Isocrates by the sarcastic use of a phrase newly-coined by him in *Against the Sophists* (13); the phrase, however, is hardly distinctive and the suggestion rests upon much supposition and presumption. See J.A. Coulter, 'Phaedrus 279a: The Praise of Isocrates', *GRBS* 8 (1967), 228-30.

τῇ χρείᾳ τοῦ βίου – unlike Isocrates, Alcidamas gives you just what you need for the real world: he is teaching ἐπὶ τέχνῃ not ἐπὶ παιδείᾳ –

Plato, *Protag.* 312b. Long after rhetoric had become a matter of the carefully composed text and <u>memoria</u> an established division of the art, improvisation continued as an art-form practised by certain poets and orators (though some 'stars' like Aristides shunned it as a stunt). See Cic. *Pro Arch.* 18; D.A. Russell, *Greek Declamation* (Cambridge,1983), 80-1.

ἐν παιδιᾳ̃ – in view of the connections in §28, Alcidamas may be thinking of Plato, *Phaedr.* 276d and 277e where Socrates talks of a written text as a παιδιά.

Odysseus
Against the treachery of Palamedes

1 – 4 PROLOGUE

I have often wondered about the motives of some who address us and who engage in quarrelsome debate which does not help the common cause. They are selfish, not caring about troublemakers and fomenting disputes about booty. The good, just man does not adopt such views. I am going to put the case fairly before you that Palamedes has committed treachery. I have had no kind of quarrel with him before and I ask you to pay particular attention because my opponent is clever.

The prologue is the first and one of the most important elements in establishing the relationship between the speaker and an audience, and this one has several features common in Greek forensic oratory. The prosecution of an individual is always more acceptable if it can be represented as a joint crusade by the prosecutor and a just audience (τὸν ἄνδρα τὸν ἀγαθὸν καὶ δίκαιον) against belligerent and selfish enemies of the common good – this group of potential trouble-makers crops up again in the epilogue. There is no direct, logical connection with Palamedes, but the juxtaposition sets the mood. The charge is clearly stated, the absence of any past ill-feeling is emphasized, and the audience is warned of the cleverness of the opponent (always a source of suspicion in the Athenian courts).

1

ὦ ἄνδρες Ἕλληνες – an obvious variation on the standard audience-tie ὦ ἄνδρες Ἀθηναῖοι. Alcidamas is not giving the pattern of a political speech, however, but of a κατηγορία in the courts. For the orators' common habit of identifying a jury with the Assembly of the people, see K.J. Dover, *Greek Popular Morality* (Oxford,1974), 292. Alcidamas tries to preserve the illusion of the imaginary situation in the Greek camp, but he constantly lapses into the contemporary, un-Homeric world (like Palamedes in Gorgias' speech, who addresses his audience as ὦ ἄνδρες κριταί – *Palam.* 28).

2

καὶ εἰ μέν τις....πλημμελεῖ – a musical metaphor – 'out of tune', cf. *OWS* §24 and 25.

εἰ δέ τις ἡμῶν.... – a reference to Homer, *Iliad* i.166-8, where Achilles complains that Agamemnon always gets the better reward (σοὶ τὸ γέρας πολὺ μεῖζον). The great quarrel between Achilles and Agamemnon is rather implausibly represented as the result of trouble-makers' efforts.

3

μήτε ἔχθρας ἰδίας φροντίζειν – probably referring both to Agamemnon and to Palamedes' own private quarrel with Odysseus. The story was that Odysseus had tried to avoid serving in the Greek army by pleading mental illness. Palamedes, however, by threatening the life of Telemachus exposed Odysseus' normal fatherly instincts and therefore his sanity, and so took away his excuse for not going to Troy – Apollod., *Epit.* 3.6-7; Hyg., *Fab.* (Rose) xcv. For a thorough survey of the relevant stories associated with Palamedes, see S. Woodford, 'Palamedes seeks revenge', *JHS* cxiv (1994), 164–9.

μήτε φιλεταιρίαν, φιλοτιμίᾳ χαρισάμενον – the MSS texts are confused and many solutions have been proposed, none entirely satisfactory. I print Radermacher's suggestion on the ground that it clearly identifies Achilles, his affection for Patroclus, and his motive for withdrawing from the war, and does not confuse this with his supposed material greed (the drawback of Avezzù's μήτε ἰδίᾳ φιλεταιρίᾳ χρησάμενον).

οὐ μὲν δή.... – there is a lacuna here and no way of telling how these words relate to it. Avezzù suggests < ἀλλ' > οὐ μὲν δή < .... > ἀλλὰ....

4

προδοσία – the degree of punishment is exaggerated for dramatic purposes, but there is probably an echo of contemporary legal practice. προδοσία was a particular crime in Athenian law. Conviction involved the loss of the right to be buried in Attica and confiscation of property, whilst the further penalty of death or exile was at the discretion of the court. It was a charge brought against several members of the Four Hundred after 411BC. See D.M. MacDowell, *The Law in Classical Athens* (London,1978), 176–9. For the probable formal legal procedures at Athens in such matters, see A.R.W. Harrison, *The Law of Athens* (Oxford,1971), ii.52–9.

οὐδεμία ἔχθρα.... – assertion of the previous absence of hostility was a rhetorical convention in the prologue. It may have been Palamedes' view of the past; it is very unlikely that Odysseus saw things this way !

οὐδ' ἐν παλαίστρᾳ οὐδ' ἐν συμποσίῳ – quite un-Homeric references to two of the dominant features of male social life in most Greek cities in the Classical and Hellenistic periods.

φιλόσοφός τε καὶ δεινός – the suggestion that the opponent was clever and professional was a subtle form of attack, playing upon a regular Athenian prejudice. Antiphon had suffered as a result of such feelings : ὑπόπτως τῷ πλήθει διὰ δόξαν δεινότητος διακείμενος – Thuc. viii.68.1. An appearance of straightforward, everyday simplicity was required by speakers in court – see K.J. Dover, *Lysias and the* Corpus Lysiacum (Berkeley and Los Angeles,1968), 155. Palamedes was a by-word for cleverness – Aristoph. *Frogs*, 1451.

5 – 7 NARRATION

As you know, we had fled to the ships .... and the enemy was attacking amidst much confusion. Diomedes and I were together, with Palamedes and Polypoites close by. An enemy archer shot at us, the arrow falling nearby, and Palamedes threw a javelin back; the archer picked up the javelin and went off to his camp. I took the arrow and gave it to Eurybates to give to Teukros for ammunition. In a pause in the fighting Eurybates showed me some incriminating writing under the feathers of the arrow, proving an agreement between Palamedes and the Trojans via Telephos. I showed this to Sthenelos and Diomedes. WITNESS STATEMENTS are then taken.

There is a swift, clear narration of the essential facts with enough witnesses to provide ample corroboration and a verbatim quote of the arrow inscription – a copy-book example of how to start the narrative part of a speech, cf. Plato, *Phaedrus* 266D....διήγησίν τινα μαρτυρίας τ' ἐπ' αὐτῇ. Although the characters and the context are Homeric, the Palamedes story itself does not occur in the *Iliad* and derives from the *Cypria*. Alcidamas' version involving the arrow and the javelin differs considerably from that of Apollodorus and conveniently removes from Odysseus any hint of duplicity; it may be Alcidamas' own invention.

5

ἐν οἵῳ κινδύνῳ ἐγενόμεθα – the context is clearly the τειχομαχία in Homer, *Iliad* xii where the Greeks are behind their ill-fated wall and the ditch protecting the ships, and are almost overwhelmed by the Trojans. The particular moment of the battle which seems to be in mind is the point of stalemate when all is in the balance – *Iliad* xii.415-24.

εἰς τὰς τάφρους – the ditch is a particular stumbling-block to the first Trojan attack – *Iliad* xii.52–9.

ἐγώ τε καὶ Διομήδης, πλησίον δ' ἦν Παλαμήδης ... – Diomedes (with the inseparable Sthenelos – §7) and Palamedes are there by pardonable dramatic licence; they are not mentioned by Homer in this episode. Polypoites, however, is prominent in the Greek defence when the Trojan Asios attacks the Greek gates and Teukros is summoned by Menestheus when Sarpedon makes his later sortie – *Iliad* xii.127ff., 343–50.

6

ἐκδραμὼν τοξότης.... – here the story parts company with the *Iliad* and with Apollodorus' version of events – *Epit.* 3.8.

Εὐρυβάτῃ δοῦναι Τεύκρῳ – Eurybates is Odysseus' κῆρυξ, also

from Ithaca, and therefore the natural intermediary – *Iliad* ii.184. The explanatory use of the infinitive to express purpose after a verb of assigning or choosing is quite usual, cf. Thuc. ii.27.

τὸν οἰστὸν ὑπὸ τοῖς πτεροῖς γράμματα ἔχοντα – the anachronism of literacy in the Homeric world is equally present in the alternative story of a letter forged by a Phrygian prisoner on Odysseus' instructions and brought to Agamemnon's attention – Apollodorus, *loc.cit.*; Hyg. *Fab.* cv (Rose).

7

'Αλέξανδρος Παλαμήδει – as if it was the start of a letter. Quotation of the actual words to be found on a piece of evidence makes a much more vivid impression than a report of them, and Alcidamas highlights this: ἡ δὲ γραφὴ ἐδήλου....ἐνεγέγραπτο μὲν ταῦτα. In the other version of the story the supposed connection is between *Priam* and Palamedes; there the opening formula of the forged letter is quoted too – PALAMEDI A PRIAMO MISSA – Hyg. *loc. cit.*

ὅσα συνέθου Τηλέφῳ – Telephos, the son of Auge and Herakles, occurs rather unexpectedly here. He was, however, a legendary figure in Mysia, the country of Alcidamas' birth (along with Teuthras who will be introduced shortly), and Alcidamas may be retailing what was to him a well-known local story – see §14 with notes. Telephos is a curiously ambiguous character; he fights with Achilles, but then, in return for the healing of a wound, guides the Greeks to Troy. Here he seems to be Palamedes' Trojan contact, and one version of the legend has him married to Laodike, the daughter of Priam, having received his education at the Trojan court – Hyg. *Fab.* ci (Rose); M. Strauss, *LIMC* vii.1,856ff.

ὅ τε πατήρ.... – the magnitude of the treachery is indicated by the promise of Priam's daughter and the character of Palamedes blackened by the fact that he had actually demanded her as his price.

οἱ λαβόντες τὸ τόξευμα – presumably Sthenelos and Diomedes; Teukros seems to have been too busy shooting.

8 – 12 PROOFS

I would have shown you the arrow but Teucer shot it back in the confusion. I must now substantiate a very serious charge against a fellow-soldier who is well thought of. None of us, in spite of being at close quarters before we arrived, saw a device on Palamedes' shield; when we got here, the trident he put there was a signal for the exchange with the Trojan soldier. The spear with writing on it must be seen as a more reliable way of sending word than using messengers. Moreover, he alone disobeyed the decree which said that captured weapons should be returned to the pool because of an armaments shortage; this deserved the death penalty. Is this not typical ? I shall show that he and his father are to blame for the present troubles, and to do this I shall have to expand my story somewhat.

The prime weakness of the prosecutor's case now clearly emerges, but in one short sentence and almost before the 'jury' has settled down after hearing the statements of the witnesses: the arrow would have clinched the matter but it is not there. How then to make a convincing case against a defendant when the crucial piece of evidence is missing ? There now follows a smoke-screen of arguments presenting what circumstantial evidence there is to try to establish the probability of guilt and the duplicitous character of the accused, and this leads on to the process of character-assassination via family history.

8

περὶ θανάτου – death was a discretionary penalty open to an Athenian jury for this offence (see §4 note), but is even more appropriate in war time.
ἄνδρα σύμμαχον ... πρότερον ἐν ὑμῖν εὐδοκιμηκότι – the prosecutor stresses the disgrace attaching to the accusation – αἰσχίστην αἰτίαν – and Palamedes' previous good record puts his shame in even starker relief, but the jury also has to feel that the prosecutor is fair-minded.

9

πρὶν ἐμβαλεῖν δεῦρο – for the use of ἐμβάλλω *sc.* στρατόν to mean 'invade', cf. Hdt. 4.125; 9.13.
πολὺν χρόνον ἐν ταὐτῷ – presumably a reference to the enforced stay at Aulis.

σημεῖον ἐν ἀσπίδι – σημεῖον is regularly used for the emblem on a shield, but the word is not found in Homer or Hesiod. Although emblems were found on the Homeric body-shield, Alcidamas is probably taking the hoplite shield of his own day for granted. The shield-device is an invariable feature of this type of shield, with the emblem either painted or applied in cutout bronze silhouette. Its original purpose seems to have been to give each person a 'logo' (as here), though later hoplites tended to show city emblems or their city's initial letter. The trident was in fact the device of Mantinea, though that seems to have no significance here. See A.M. Snodgrass, *Arms and Armor of the Greeks* (Baltimore and London,1999), 54–5 and 67.

τίνος ἕνεκα; – the rhetorical question is a simple but effective device. The answering purpose clause becomes a more emphatic statement and gives the appearance of a revelation; the audience is brought into the argument.

10

εἰκότως – there is not a shred of evidence about what was on the spear, and so Alcidamas has to admit that he is now dealing in probabilities. Probability argument was one of the features of early rhetoric much cultivated by Gorgias, though used more sparingly by his pupils. See M. Gagarin, 'Probability and Persuasion' in I. Worthington ed., *Persuasion* (London, 1994), 51–5.

πιστὰ γάρ....καὶ μὴ δι᾽ ἀγγέλων – literacy has clearly arrived: writing is to be trusted, human messengers are not.

11

ψήφισμα ἡμῖν ἐγένετο – the word ψήφισμα belongs naturally to Athenian political life and is quite un-Homeric.

διὰ τὸ σπανίοις αὐτοῖς χρῆσθαι ἡμᾶς – for the idiom, cf. Thuc. vii.4.6 – τῷ τε γὰρ ὕδατι σπανίῳ χρώμενοι....

βέλη ἀνελόμενος πέντε – in the MSS the word τοξεύειν follows πέντε. MacDowell's ingenious conjecture τοξευθείς makes sense and is adopted by Avezzù. However, the two participle phrases in tandem are then very awkward, and οὐδὲ ἕν loses its significance. Sauppe and Blass are probably right simply to omit τοξεύειν.

δικαίως ἄν μοι δοκεῖ θανάτῳ ζημιωθῆναι – the death

penalty for treachery seems fair enough; to invoke it for failure to turn in captured weapons may seem incongruous, but it was standard practice for prosecutors to demand the death penalty as an *ad terrorem* device, even for comparatively minor offences. See K.J. Dover, *Greek Popular Morality* (Oxford,1974), 289–90.

12

τοῦ φρονήματος αὐτοῦ....ὃς τυγχάνει φιλοσοφῶν – there is clearly a lacuna and Avezzù suggests that something like ἐστιν ἀπολελειμμένα filled the gap. Other suggestions have been made, but, beyond the fact that the sentence has the character of a general summing-up, no certainty is possible.

αἴτιον γεγονότα – to make Palamedes and his father, Nauplios, responsible for the expedition against Troy as well usefully extends the scope of Palamedes' guilt. Vague and more general suggestions of culpability – however poorly substantiated – were common practice in the courts.

διὰ μακροτέρων λόγων – the wording of the explanation of the long account of family history indicates a demonstration of the technique of μακρολογία – extending the subject-matter. See note on *OWS*, § 23.

12(end) – 16

Palamedes's father, Nauplios, a poor fisherman, did much damage to the Greeks. Aleos, king of Tegea, having been warned by Delphi that, if his daughter, Auge, had a child, that child would kill his sons, made her a priestess of Athena. However, Herakles on a visit saw her and was carried away by drink. When she became pregnant, Aleos sent for Nauplios and told him to drown her in the sea. Nauplios, however, disobeyed. A baby, Telephos was born, and Nauplios, further ignoring Aleos' instructions, gave mother and child to Teuthras, king of Mysia, who took her as his wife and, being childless, adopted Telephos, sending him to be educated at Troy with King Priam.

The story does not seem at first sight very relevant, but it emphasizes that Palamedes had a lowly and unreliable father in Nauplios who did much damage to the Greeks and, second, that Telephos, evidently Palamedes' chief contact on the Trojan side, was the result of Nauplios' deliberate disobedience. Alcidamas does not mention the brush Telephos had with Achilles, the wound he sustained, and the manner of its healing (which led to Telephos giving guidance to the Greeks on their way to Troy); Telephos is firmly identified by Alcidamas with the Trojans.

13

πατήρ ἐστι πένης – Palamedes was the son of Nauplios and Klymene. Klymene was one of the two daughters of Katreus, son of Minos and Pasiphae. She had been given to Nauplios to sell because of a prophecy that one of Katreus' children would kill him, but Nauplios took her as his wife instead – Apollod. 3.2. The parallelism between this and the story of Aleos and Auge which follows may suggest that Alcidamas imported the idea of a prophecy given to Aleos; it is not found in any of the other sources.

πλείστους τῶν ʽΕλλήνων ἠφάνικεν – this seems to be an awkward and anachronistic reference to what happened after the Trojan War. To avenge Palamedes' death, Nauplios set false fire-beacons near Cape Kaphareus in Euboea to misdirect the Greeks returning from Troy (who had already suffered from a storm); the fleet was wrecked and Nauplios killed many of the survivors. Alcidamas also throws in looting as an extra villainy – Apollod. *Epit.* 6.7–8; Hyg. *Fab.* cxvi (Rose); Eur. *Hel.* 767, 1126ff.

πανουργίας τε οὐδεμίας λείπεται – perhaps to give a hint to the audience of Nauplios' other activity in trying to persuade the wives of the Greek warriors to be unfaithful – Apollod. *Epit.* 6.8–9.

γνώσεσθε δὲ – the promise is not fulfilled and Alcidamas does not refer to these events again. However, Nauplios' character is already blackened before the narrative proper begins.

14

ʼΑλέῳ γάρ.... – there are two elements to the story of Aleos, Auge and Telephos (Pausanias found both happily co-existing in Tegea – 8.48.7). There are also considerable variations within the two story strands and they become conflated. In the first strand Herakles has his way with Auge and she has a baby, Telephos (the exact point in the story at which she has the baby varies). The baby is then exposed on Mt. Parthenion and is nurtured by a deer and later adopted and given a name by some shepherds. This version seems to belong primarily to Arcadia, and in Pausanias' day a *temenos* to Telephos still existed on Mt. Parthenion – Paus. 8.54.6. In the second strand which

Pausanias found in Hecataeus and which Euripides used, Auge becomes pregnant and is put with her baby into a chest and sent out to sea. The chest makes a miraculous voyage to Mysia (or, in another version, Auge is given by Nauplios to some Carians who take her to Mysia), where Auge and her baby are brought to Teuthras who rules in the valley of the river Kaïkos. Since he is childless, he marries her and adopts her son, Telephos, who is later sent to the court of King Priam to be educated. This strand makes the transition between Arcadia and Mysia, and it was largely the origin of both the dramatic treatments of the story (Aeschylus, Sophocles and Euripides each wrote more than one play using the myth) and its adoption by the Attalids as a foundation-legend for Pergamum (the Telephos frieze on the Great Altar being its most conspicuous manifestation) – Apollod. 2.7.4, 3.9.1; Hyg. *Fab.* xcix (Rose); Diod. Sic. 4.33.7–12; Strabo xiii.69; Paus. 8.4.9, 47.4, 48.7. For further discussion, see J.G. Frazer ed. and trans., *Apollodorus: The Library* (Loeb, London and New York), i.252ff. n. 2; A Szantyr, 'Die Telephostrilogie des Sophocles', *Philologus* xcii (1939), 287–324; E.V. Hansen, *The Attalids of Pergamum* (Ithaca and London, 1971), 4–13.

Alcidamas uses both strands of the story and is obviously specially concerned with the role of Nauplios, Palamedes' father, who regularly occurs as the agent used by Aleos to try to get rid of the baby (and the mother in some versions); Nauplios' unreliability and duplicity are deliberately played up. Telephos is also prominent (to tie in with the message on the arrow) and is associated by implication with Priam and Troy. For the localization of legends associated with Auge and Teuthras, see Strabo xiii.68–9.

ἱέρειαν τῆς ᾽Αθηνᾶς – in Apollodorus' version (3.9.1) Auge is a priestess of Athena too, but she both has her baby in Athena's precinct and hides it there.

ἐπ᾽ ᾽Αυγέαν – this is clearly the revenge expedition which Herakles later undertook following Augeas' failure to pay for the cleansing of the stables.

15

ὑπὸ μέθης – an ungallant and gratuitous motivation which does not occur elsewhere but which fits Herakles' mythological profile. By Pausanias' time the fountain beside which Auge lost her virtue was one of the 'sights' of Tegea – Paus. 8.47.4.

16

ἐν τῷ Παρθενίῳ ὄρει – Diodorus Siculus has the rather crude story of Auge pretending to go behind a bush, and then giving birth – 4.33.9. Elsewhere the baby is either born on the mountain or in Tegea.

ἀμελήσας δὲ.... – to remind us of Nauplios' unreliability and disobedience.

ἀπέδοτο....ἐς Μυσίαν – Avezzù believes that Nauplios merely 'entrusts' Auge and her mother to Teuthras ('e li affidò'). However, there is no need to fight shy of the normal meaning of the middle; the fact that Nauplios sold them is an extra turn of the screw. For the destination of sale following ἀποδίδομαι, cf. Hdt. ii.56 – τὴν δὲ ἐς τὴν Ἑλλάδα ἀπέδοντο....

ἐπονομάσας Τήλεφον – Apollodorus offers some fanciful etymology, saying it was the shepherds on Mt. Parthenion who gave Telephos his name, deriving it from θηλή and ἔλαφος because he was suckled by a deer – Apollod. 2.7.4; 3.9.1.

17 – 19

Paris wanted to visit Greece because of a desire to see Delphi and because he had heard of Helen's beauty and the manner of Telephos' birth. At this point the children of Molos arrived in Sparta asking Menelaus to settle an inheritance dispute and he therefore departed, leaving instructions to his wife and her brothers that generous hospitality should be available to their guests. Paris then seduced Helen and left, taking with him as much as he could. Did you summon help or raise the alarm? No – you looked the other way as Greeks were insulted by barbarians.

By the start of this section the audience/jury may feel with some justification that it has lost sight of Palamedes altogether and the suggestion that the circumstances of Telephos' birth (in Arcadia !) supplied one of the motives for Paris' visit to Sparta is a pretty weak and clumsy link. The audience-prompt – 'Well, so what happens ?' – may be an unconscious symptom of a wandering argument. However, the scene shifts from the local stories of Tegea and Mysia to the more familiar central cause of the Trojan War and Palamedes' part in it; having established his father's lowly origins and duplicitous, greedy character, Odysseus now accuses Palamedes of wrong-doing by inaction; the best of a bad job for a prosecutor.

17

τό τε ἱερὸν τὸ ἐν Δελφοῖς.... – the motives for Paris' visit to Greece are usually unexplained. Apart from the obvious (δηλονότι) attraction of seeing Helen, a visit to Delphi was a common reason for visits from abroad (though usually with some purpose). Curiosity about Telephos' origins is an unlikely motive and an awkward link to Aleos, Auge and Nauplios (unless it is assumed that Telephos' tales of Greece had whetted Paris's appetite for further acquaintance).

ἐν δὲ τῷ καιρῷ τούτῳ – καιρός here has its full meaning of 'this critical moment'.

οἱ Μόλου παῖδες ... – this version of the story is not found elsewhere. The usual reason for Menelaus' ill-timed visit to Crete is the funeral of his father-in-law, Katreus – Apollod. *Epit.* 3.3. Molos was said to be the bastard son of Deucalion and therefore the half-brother of Katreus – Apollod. 3.3.1. He was also the father of Meriones who was presumably one of the sons who came to see Menelaus about their disputed inheritance – Homer, *Iliad* x.269; xiii.249; Hyg. *Fab.* xcvii (Rose); Diod. Sic. 5.79.4.

18

ἐπιστείλας τῇ γυναικὶ – Menelaus is presented as friendly and hospitable, cf. his reception of Telemachus in *Od.* iv.31ff.

τοῖς ἀδελφοῖς – Castor and Polydeuces. They too are associated with hospitality in the customs of θεοξενία, though as recipients rather than donors. See M.P. Nilsson, *Geschichte der griechischen Religion* (München, 1967), i.409.

ἀποιχομένου....τὴν γυναῖκα – the reading here has been suspected and various solutions suggested. MacDowell convincingly proposed ἀποιχομένου for the MSS ἀφικομένου (Avezzù wrongly credits him with defending the MSS here).

19

ἔστιν ὅπου ἀντέλαβου.... – the sudden address in the second person brings Palamedes into the limelight with something of a jolt, especially as narrative takes over again in §20. Alcidamas' three possibilities for action – getting hold of someone, shouting to the neighbours, and finding help – seem much more appropriate to the kind of domestic incident with which Antiphon, Lysias and other logographers were customarily concerned; when Paris had left with Helen and the stolen goods, there was little Palamedes could have done, and, according to Euripides, Helen made no attempt to cry for help, even though there were people at hand like Castor and Polydeuces – *Troades*, 999–1001. However, the appeal to insulted Hellenic consciousness partially papers over the cracks.

20 – 21

When Menelaus discovered the abduction, he sent us out to various cities to ask for arms and help. He sent Palamedes to Oinopion in Chios and to Kinyras in Cyprus, but Palamedes persuaded Kinyras not to join the expedition, receiving many presents from him. Palamedes gave Agamemnon a worthless breastplate but kept the rest for himself. He brought a message back from Kinyras that Cyprus would send 100 ships, and you see that not one has come. So Palamedes deserves the death penalty – a clever man who has been devising the basest treachery.

The story of the recruiting expedition has been modified by Alcidamas to give Palamedes a prominent and treacherous role. He has been made responsible for Kinyras' failure to contribute ships to the expedition (though the traditional story suggests that Kinyras was the devious one), and he is accused of short-changing Agamemnon over the breastplate (though Homer suggests the opposite). Treachery and cheating are useful ingredients for a character-assassination.

20

εἰς Χίον πρὸς 'Οινοπίωνα – Oinopion, the son of Dionysus and Ariadne, was said to have founded the city of Chios – Paus. 7.4.7-9. His alleged introduction of wine-making to the island is obviously derived from his name – Diod. Sic. 5.79.1. See O. Touchefeu-Meynier, *LIMC* viii.1 (Suppl.), 920–1. Chios became one of the wealthiest of the Ionian cities – Thuc. viii.24.4, 40.1 – this is doubtless the reason for Alcidamas sending Palamedes there as well as Cyprus.

εἰς Κύπρον πρὸς Κινύραν.... – in Apollodorus' version of the story (*Epit.* 3.9), Menelaus goes to Cyprus himself taking Odysseus and Talthybius (no mention of Palamedes). Kinyras gives a present of breastplates (here plural) to Agamemnon in his absence, and promises to send 50 ships. In the event he only sends one, keeping to the letter of his promise by making 49 pottery ship-models and putting them in the sea (by the time Eustathius wrote his Commentary, this story had been charmingly extended by including pottery crews on the ships – M. Van der Valk ed., *Eustathii Commentarii ad Homeri Iliadem pertinentes* (Leiden,1979), iii.139, §827).

ὁ δὲ < .... > – a lacuna is not grammatically required, but there is no mention of what Palamedes may have got up to on Chios with Oinopion; Avezzù may be right in suspecting that something has fallen out.

ἀποπλέων ᾤχετο – another example of the pleonastic habit which so annoyed Aristotle.

21

θώρακα ὅστις οὐδενὸς ἄξιος ἦν – Alcidamas openly contradicts Homer, who goes out of his way to describe in detail the very elaborate breastplate with inlays of enamel, gold and tin and with a snake design which Kinyras gave to Agamemnon – *Iliad* xi.19–28. For speculation about the exact nature of the decoration, see M.M. Willcock ed., *The Iliad of Homer* (London,1978), i.296–7.

22 – 28

He has, moreover, made deceitful claims to the young in shamelessly saying that he is the inventor of military formations, alphabetic letters, numbers, measures, weights, draughts, dice, music, coinage and fire-beacons. In fact, Nestor and Menestheus made use of troop-formations, Orpheus invented writing, Linos discovered music, Musaeus numbers and the Phoenicians invented coinage. All these were before his time. Draughts and dice have both been bad influences and have the most unfortunate results. Fire-beacons he did invent in order to harm us and benefit our enemies. A true man is loyal to his commanders, obeys orders and pleases the majority, and his virtue is to do good to friends and harm to enemies. This man has done the opposite: helping enemies and harming friends.

The focus now shifts to intellectual dishonesty. Having established an act of blatant treachery, a questionable and lowly family background leading (albeit indirectly) to a disastrous war, cowardly inaction at a moment of crisis, gross self-seeking involving cheating the commander-in-chief and weakening the whole expedition, Alcidamas/Odysseus now moves in on Palamedes' legendary cleverness and reputation as an inventor. The tactics are two-fold: to prove some of his claims openly false, and to show that the others, even if true, have brought nothing but trouble (with a glance at the later events at Cape Kaphareus). The whole thing is rounded off by standing the conventional Greek definition of the behaviour of a good man on its head.

22

ἐξαπατῶν τοὺς νέους – the rhetoricians and sophists, like all teachers, evidently had to be wary of such charges; Socrates was not alone.

φάσκων τάξεις ἐξευρηκέναι πολεμικάς ... – this impressive list of discoveries adds three (music, coinage and dice) to the similar list in [Gorgias] *Palamedes* 28ff. Stesichorus and Euripides give Palamedes credit for inventing writing (*fr.* 213 – *PMG* p.209); on a more modest scale he is said to have invented some letters of the alphabet (11 according to Hyg. *Fab.* cclxxvii (Rose); 4 according to Pliny, *NH* 7.192). He is also said to have invented draughts and dicing to while away the time during the Trojan War – Paus. 2.20.3. See Avezzù, 81 for a table setting out the various inventions with which Palamedes was credited and their sources. The only three not mentioned by Alcidamas are fortifications, astronomy, and provisions.

23

Νέστωρ γὰρ....ἐν φάλαγγι καὶ τάξει – the phalanx usually signifies the hoplite soldiers (as distinct from other types of fighting men) in battle order. See P. Connolly, *Greece and Rome at War* (London, 1981),

37ff.; J.K. Anderson, *Military Theory and Practice in the Age of Xenophon* (Berkeley,1970), 106 and 109. For a detailed survey of the archaeological evidence, see H.L. Lorimer, 'The Hoplite Phalanx' *Ann.BSA* xlii (1947), 76–138. In Homer's three references to Nestor's fight with the Centaurs at the wedding of Peirithoos and Hippodameia, there is no hint of organized tactics despite the distinguished company of warriors; it is more a matter of a brawl – *Iliad* i.262–8; ii.742–4; *Od.* xxi.295–304.

Μενεσθεὺς δὲ πρῶτος.... – Menestheus became king of Athens while Theseus was in Hades and subsequently took 50 ships to Troy; he is the rather surprising leader of the Athenian contingent in the Greek army. According to Alcidamas, it was during his reign that Eumolpos made an attack on Athens with Thracian troops. The traditional story said firmly that the attack of Eumolpos, whether self-generated or prompted by Eleusis, happened during the reign of Erechtheus (who was told by Delphi that he must sacrifice his daughter to gain the final victory) – see Eur. *Erechth.* fr. 360, 40–9; C. Collard, M.J. Cropp and K.H. Lee, *Euripides: Selected Fragmentary Plays* (Warminster, 1995), i.148–152; Apollod. 3.15.4; Lycurg. *In Leocrat.* 98. It looks as though Menestheus has been rather dragged in to the argument: he is not a prominent figure nor is he anywhere associated with tactical military developments. He was, however, according to one story, the legendary founder of Alcidamas' home town, Elaia – Strabo 13.3.5; Steph. Byz. s.v.'Ελαία – and this may account for his appearance here.

τάξεις καὶ λόχους – the λόχος was supposedly the formation from which the phalanx originated; it consisted of four blocks of 32 men (in the Spartan pattern). See Connolly, *op.cit.*, 37.

24

γράμματα μὲν δὴ πρῶτος 'Ορφεὺς ἐξήνεγκε – the invention of the Greek letters and fully alphabetic writing was more commonly ascribed to Cadmus and the Phoenicians. See J.N. Coldstream, *Geometric Greece* (London, 1977), 295–302; W.V. Harris, *Ancient Literacy* (Cambridge, Mass. and London,1989), 45–6. Myth, though, deals with universals, and perhaps 'writing' rather than 'Greek alphabetic writing' is what is meant; the search for the origins of writing is another story – see R. Harris, *The Origin of Writing* (London,1986).

Μουσάων....Θρῆκες ἔθηκαν – the grave of Orpheus and his cult were not located in Thrace but in Pieria to the north-east of Mt. Olympus. In no other source is Orpheus said to be the teacher of Herakles and the manner of his death described here is not at all the usual one. The epigram may well go back in part to a monument somewhere in Macedonia, for Diogenes Laertius (*Prologue* 1.5) recorded the following epigram from Dion in Macedonia:

Θρήϊκα χρυσολύρην τῇδ' 'Ορφέα Μοῦσαι ἔθαψαν
ὅν κτάνεν ὑψιμέδων Ζεὺς ψολόεντι βέλει.

Pausanias also reports that in Macedonia 'some say' that Orpheus was killed by a thunderbolt, divine-sent (9.30.5). See I.M. Linforth, *The Arts of Orpheus* (Berkeley,1941), 15–6; ibid., 'Two Notes on the legend of Orpheus', *TAPA* lxii (1931), 5–11.

25

μουσικὴν δὲ Λίνος – Linos was the name of both a mythical person and a song; the song is as old as Homer – *Iliad* xviii.570. He was a composer, teacher and performer, and was said to have invented the θρῆνος – Herakl. Pont. in [Plut.] *De mus.* 3. He taught Herakles and was killed by him in one version of his life story – Apollod. 2.63. In another version he was killed because he claimed to be as good a singer as Apollo – Paus. 9.29.6ff. It has been suggested that Linos acquired his human identity as the personification of the dirge; however, only here is it claimed that he invented music as a whole. See J. Boardman, *LIMC* vi.1, 290.

ἀριθμούς γε μὴν Μουσαῖος – Musaeus is something of a puzzle, although he is regularly listed from the later fifth century BC as one of the ancient sages – Hdt. 7.6; 8.96; 9.43; Aristoph. *Frogs* 1033; Plato, *Rep.* 363b. However, as West says, '...there are no myths about him. His life is a blank. He is nothing but a source of verses'. His claim to being the inventor of numbers appears to rest on the fact that the two lines of verse quoted contain them ! The fact that he is here associated with the Eumolpidai and called an Athenian may be the result of his adoption by Eleusis before the end of the fifth century BC as head of the genealogy of the Eumolpidai and the father of Eumolpus. See M.L. West, *The Orphic Poems* (Oxford, 1983), 39–44.

ὄρθιον ἐξαμερὲς.... – the line is attributed to Orpheus and the Pythia as well as to Musaeus and clearly refers to the hexameter with its six feet and twenty four *morae*. It may be a claim for the invention of the hexameter rather than for the discovery of numbers; Democritus credited Musaeus with the invention of the hexameter – DK 68 B 15; West, *op.cit.*, 232–3.

ὡς δεκάτην.... – the meaning and provenance of the line are obscure; it plainly has no connection with the hexameter and is only included because of the numbers.

26

νομίσματα δὲ οὐ Φοίνικες ἐξεῦρον – the Phoenicians are nowhere else said to have invented coinage; other claimants to the discovery were Pheidon of Argos, Demodike, wife of the Phrygian Midas, the Athenians, Erichthonios and Lykos and the people of Naxos – Pollux, *Onom.* ix.83. There is little doubt both from literary and archaeological evidence that coinage began round about 600 BC in the area of Asia Minor where Ionian Greeks and Lydians were in contact. See I. Carradice and M. Price, *Coinage in the Greek World* (London,1988), 20–9.

ἐξ ὁλοσφύρου γὰρ.... – the text is uncertain and Reiske virtually declared *locus desperatus*. Despair need not be total however for the general sense is clear. The passage describes the essentials of ancient Greek coin manufacture: first, the production of flans of equal weight from pure metal ingots(?), and second, the stamping of the type (the χαρακτήρ was the upper die which was struck, the lower being set in the anvil); the value of the coin corresponded to its weight. ὁλόσφυρον – 'hammered as a whole' – occurs only here and must mean something like 'ingot', for the flans were never cut from beaten metal. Exactly how the ἴσος μερισμός was made so accurately is uncertain, despite modern experimentation. See G.K. Jenkins, *Ancient Greek Coins* (London,1990), 4–5; C.T. Seltman, *Greek Coins* (London,1955), 21–2.

27

καὶ κύβους αὖ....καταναλίσκεται παραχρῆμα – perhaps a small example of μακρολογία; there is no special reason for singling out dice, except of course that they are a focus for further moralizing disapproval.

28

ἐπὶ τῷ ἡμετέρῳ κακῷ – another reference to the deliberate wrecking at Cape Kaphareus, cf. §13.

τούς τε φίλους εὖ ποιοῦντα.... – for many examples of this commonly-acknowledged standard of Greek behaviour and attitude, see K.J. Dover, *Greek Popular Morality* (Oxford,1974), 180ff.

29 EPILOGUE

I believe you should think carefully now he is in your hands. If you are sorry for him and let him go, indiscipline will result, and individuals will start to commit offences knowing that they can get away with it. Vote for your own interests and make him an example.

Odysseus' epilogue is a copy-book exercise – short, and playing upon the universal fear that relaxing the rules of society will encourage more widespread wrong-doing. It is a plea frequently used and particularly apt in a democratic society conscious of its collective responsibility, and the orators are understandably fond of it as a closing sentiment.

29

κοινῇ σκεψαμένους βουλεύσασθαι – people meeting to hear and discuss important matters soon acquire a sense of group identity; it does no harm for the advocate to show that he understands.

εἰ δὲ κατελεήσαντες....πειράσονται ἀδικεῖν – the idea that a wrong decision in the case will harm the city or the common interest, or will encourage wrong-doing (or even make for an uncomfortable home life – [Dem.] 59.112) is one of the standard ingredients in court-room epilogues, cf. Lysias 12.35; 22.19–20; 27.7; 30.23; Dem. 50.66; 54.43; [Gorgias] *Palam.* 36; Andoc. 1.140.

The Fragments

The Messenian Speech

1. The text is given by an anonymous commentator on Aristot. *Rhet.* i.
1373b18. Aristotle says that Alcidamas gives an example in his *Messenian
Speech* of the universal kind of law based on nature, but with no quotation.
The commentator gives Alcidamas' actual words: ὑπερ Μεσσηνίων ἀπο-
στατησάντων Λακεδαιμονίων καὶ μὴ πειθομένων δουλεύειν
μελετᾷ καὶ λέγει 'Αλκιδάμας – H. Rabe ed., *Commentaria in
Aristotelem Graeca* (Berlin,1896), xxi.2. p.74. Aristotle refers to the speech
here and at *Rhet.* ii.1397a as if it was well-known. Whether it is a true
festival speech or a piece written for display inspired by a great event is
unknown (Brzoska, 1536 suspected the latter because of the commentator's
use of the word μελετᾷ).
Whatever the occasion of the speech, this is a noble and universal statement,
and Guthrie regarded it as a landmark in the articulation of a great principle –
'surely a great step forward in the history of human relations has been taken'
(W.K.C. Guthrie, *The Sophists* (Cambridge,1971), 160).

2. This is quoted directly by Aristotle in *Rhet.* ii.1397a as an example of an
enthymeme working from opposites. Quintilian gives what is clearly a loose
Latin translation of Alcidamas' sentence – *si malorum causa bellum est, erit
emendatio pax* – but includes it *ex eo genere quod ἐπαγωγὴν Graeci
vocant, Cicero inductionem* – 5.10.73.

Quotations of doubtful origin

3. This is quoted by Aristotle in *Rhet.* ii.1398b as an example of an
enthymeme working from induction. The list is a conventional one, though it
is strange to find Homer mentioned as not being a citizen of Chios, a place
usually reckoned as one of the strong claimants to being his birthplace. I have
omitted the words καὶ 'Ιταλιῶται Πυθαγόραν which in most texts of

Aristotle follow φιλόλογοι ὄντες, persuaded by R. Kassel, *Der Text der Aristotelischen Rhetorik* (Berlin,1971), 139–40. Avezzù prints this quotation and No.4 under the heading of the *Book of Nature* but there is no justification for this, and, if anything, guesswork might locate them in a prologue to the *Mouseion*.

4. This follows on from No.3 above in the text of Aristotle. It therefore seems to be a continuation of the quotation from Alcidamas and may be so, but the the tenor of it changes the pattern of argument very abruptly and Kassel (*loc.cit.*) suggested that it might be a later addition by Aristotle himself; others have suggested a preceding lacuna. The attribution to Alcidamas is therefore in some doubt.

The 'Theban rulers' may perhaps be Epaminondas and Pelopidas.

5. This is quoted by Diogenes Laertius in addition to describing Protagoras' achievements. Protagoras is said to have made a different classification: εὐχωλήν, ἐρώτησιν, ἀπόκρισιν, ἐντόλην, 'wish, question, answer, command'. Others made a sevenfold classification: διήγησιν, ἐρώτησιν, ἀπόκρισιν, ἐντολήν, ἀπαγγελίαν, εὐχωλήν, κλῆσιν, 'narration, question, answer, command, report, wish, calling' – Diog. Laert. 9.54 = *Suda* iv.247 (Adler). Such divisions may be attempts to classify language for rhetorical purposes; they may also at the same time be early searchings after grammatical categories, for the tendency to confuse semantics and forms of language in theories of diction bedevilled attempts to systematise grammar for a considerable time. See M. Frede, 'Principles of Stoic Grammar' in J.M. Rist ed., *The Stoics* (Berkeley,1978), 45ff.

6. For this very Aristotelian idea, cf. *Rhet.* i.1355b ff. The definition is actually attributed to οἱ περὶ τὸν 'Αλκιδάμαντα – *Prolegomena in Hermogenes περὶ στασέων* in H. Rabe ed., *Prolegomenon Sylloge* (Leipzig,1931), 192 ll. 10–11. For a similar definition from an anonymous source, see Rabe, *op.cit.*, 232 ll. 15–16.

Aristotle – *Rhetoric* Book iii

7 – 25. All these phrases are quoted by Aristotle in *Rhet.* iii, 1406a–b as examples of different features of style of which he disapproved. The section contains phrases from Lykophron and Gorgias, but most of the examples are taken from Alcidamas and it must be assumed that Aristotle found his style particularly irritating. There are four sub-divisions giving the main categories of short-coming. The criticisms are introduced under the general heading of τὰ ψυχρά, 'coldnesses' or 'frigidities' of style. What they have in common seems to be a dislike of a strained or unduly artificial, poetic use of words. 'Coldness' – a style which has no warmth and vigour – became a regular term of stylistic criticism, probably under the influence of Aristotle – see [Long.], *De sub.* ch. 3-4. It was though a less technical term in pre-Aristotelian usage: Aristoph., *Thesm.* 170, 848; Plato, *Euthyd.* 284e; *Laws* 802d.

7 – 10 come under the heading of words with two components (ἔν τε διπλοῖς ὀνόμασιν). No.7 is surely a paraphrase of *Iliad* i.103–4. Of the four doublet words quoted, πυρίχρων occurs only here and, though colourful, hardly seems excessive; τελεσφόρος is a regular Homeric word in the phrase τελεσφόρον εἰς ἐνιαυτόν (e.g. *Iliad* xix.32; *Od.* iv.86), and beyond that seems confined to tragic diction; κυανόχρως occurs here and twice in Euripides and actually seems rather good for the bottom of the sea. The objection seems to be that compound adjectives of this kind have a poetic flavour (ποιητικὰ διὰ τὴν δίπλωσιν φαίνεται).

11 – 13 illustrate Alcidamas' use of strange or foreign words (τὸ χρῆσθαι γλώτταις); for γλῶττα in this sense, see Aristot., *Poet.* 1457b. Here again it seems to be words in the poetic domain which are criticised: ἄθυρμα is Homeric and poetic (Pindar and Bacchylides); ἀτασθαλία is again Homeric (but only in the plural in Homer) and poetic, though Herodotus uses it once; τεθηγμένος is largely poetic, though Xenophon uses it occasionally. On all these, see LSJ. No. 13 certainly seems rather extravagant with metaphors from wine-mixing and knife-sharpening combined.

14 – 23 demonstrate Alcidamas' tendency to pack his style with obvious

epithets (ἐν τοῖς ἐπιθέτοις τὸ ἢ μακροῖς ἢ πυκνοῖς χρῆσθαι). Aristotle expands his criticism a little: 'for he uses epithets not as a sweet but as the main course, so dense and large and obvious are they' (οὐ γὰρ ἡδύσματι χρῆται ἀλλ᾽ ὡς ἐδέσματι τοῖς ἐπιθέτοις....). This perhaps has an echo in Dionysius of Halicarnassus' description of Alcidamas as παχύτερον ὄντα τὴν λέξιν καὶ κενότερον – *Isaeus* 19. It is understandable that such a clear thinker as Aristotle should be annoyed by the kind of searching for expressiveness demonstrated in these phrases; however, one man's meat.... , and Cicero admired Alcidamas' *ubertas* – *Tusc. Disp.* i.48.116. Effective oratory is not always concise. The main objection seems to be that using language proper to poetry produces a lack of clarity (διαλύει τὸ σαφὲς τῷ ἐπισκοτεῖν). No.21 clearly refers to *Od.* vi.128–9.

24 – 25 (and 11) illustrate a tendency to inappropriate metaphor, and again it is hard to see the force of Aristotle's objection. It may be fanciful to describe philosophy as the bulwark of the laws, but surely allowable on a public occasion, and the phrase about the *Odyssey* is quite memorable and attractive. Poetic diction can hardly be the problem here. κάτοπτρον in No. 25 perhaps stresses not only the fidelity of the *Odyssey* to human life, but the fact that it is a medium which allows the contemplation of human life too, cf. Xen. *Symp.* 4.6.

All the phrases quoted by Aristotle do not at first sight have any obvious link or sequence, but Solmsen in a piece of virtuoso scholarship suggested that Aristotle may have been following a practice which can be demonstrated from *Rhet.* iii.1409b ff. and 1411b where quotations from Isocrates are given in the order in which they occur in the original work. Solmsen suggested that the quotations from Alcidamas too might be taken in sequence from a single work. If this was so, he concluded that the work was concerned with poetry and the quotations point to a short section on epic and another on tragedy, the two genres representative of high poetry. The tragedy, he suggested, was a so-called *Leidenschafttragödie* of the early Euripidean type (he demonstrated – as an example – how some quotations might fit a discussion of *Medea*). Finally he proposed that the work which Aristotle was excerpting may have been the prologue to the *Mouseion*, and that the nature of poetry and its effects were discussed in it. The argumentation is ingenious, and it is indeed

Alcidamas

tempting to try to make sense of a sequence of fragments, but other scenarios could be imagined and Solmsen's reconstruction must remain an attractive possibility. See F. Solmsen, 'Drei Rekonstruktionen zur antiken Rhetorik und Poetik', *Hermes* 67 (1932), 133–44.

The *Mouseion*

26. Stobaeus 4.52.22 quotes this couplet from Alcidamas' *Mouseion*. The same couplet is found in Theognis and the same versified sentiments can be found in a number of other places – see M.L. West, *Iambi et Elegi Graeci* (Oxford,1989), i.194, no.425 with refs. in the *apparatus*. There is no reason to believe that it was not a quotation used in the *Mouseion*.

27. For the sake of easy, normal reading I have printed the text of Michigan papyrus 2754 with prose and verse conventionally separated. The text of the papyrus with original line division and line numbers is as follows:

οἱ δὲ ὁρῶντες αὐτὸν ἐσχεδίασαν τόνδε τὸν
στίχον· 'ὅσσ' ἕλομεν λιπόμεσθ', ὅσσ' οὐχ ἕλομεν
φερόμεσθα.' ὁ δὲ δυνάμενος εὑρεῖν τὸ λεχθὲν ἤρετο αὐτοὺς ὅ τι λέγοιεν. οἱ δὲ ἔφασαν ἐ-
φ' ἁλιείαν οἰχόμενοι ἀγρεῦσαι μὲν οὐδέν, καθή-   5
μενοι δὲ φθειρίζεσθαι, τῶν δὲ φθειρῶν οὓς ἔλαβον αὐτοῦ καταλιπεῖν, οὓς δὲ οὐκ ἔλαβον ἐν
τοῖς τρίβωσιν ἐν[θ]' ἀποφέρειν. ἀναμνησθεὶς δὲ
τοῦ μαντείου, ὅτι ἡ καταστροφὴ αὐτῷ τοῦ
βίου ἧκεν, ποιεῖ εἰς ἑαυτὸν ἐπίγραμμα τόδε·   10
ἐνθάδε τὴν ἱερὴν κεφαλὴν κατὰ γαῖα κάλυψε ἀνδρῶν ἡρώων κοσμήτορα θεῖον Ὅμηρον.'
καὶ ἀναχωρῶν πηλοῦ ὄντος ὀλισθάνει καὶ πεσὼν ἐπὶ πλευρὰν οὕτως, φασίν, ἐτελεύτησεν.
περὶ τούτου μὲν οὖν ποιεῖσθαι τὴν ἀρετὴν πει-   15
ρασόμεθα, μάλιστα δ' ὁρῶντες τοὺς ἱστορικοὺς θαυμαζομένους. Ὅμηρος γοῦν διὰ τοῦτο καὶ ζῶν
καὶ ἀποθανὼν τετίμηται παρὰ πᾶσιν ἀνθρώποις. ταύτη[ν] οὖν αὐτῷ τῆς παιδιᾶς χάριν ἀ-
ποδίδο[ντες τὸ γέ]νος αὐτοῦ καὶ τὴν ἄλλην ποί-   20
ησιν δι' ἀκ[ριβ]είας μνήμης τοῖς βουλομέ-

νοις φι[λοκαλ]εῖν τῶν Ἑλλήνων εἰς τὸ κοινὸν
παραδῶμεν.
       Ἀλκι]δάμαντος
      Περὶ Ὁμήρου.   25

There is no doubt that ll. 1–14 correspond to the end of the *Contest,* 326; the same riddle is described (the line of verse is identical), and Homer comes to the same end in the same way. The epigrams are nearly identical (καλύπτει in the *Contest,* κάλυψε in the papyrus). The riddle and most of the story of Homer's death are also to be found in the extant Lives of Homer, and the riddle was known to Heraclitus (B 56 DK). However, the correspondence is not close enough to suggest versions of the same text. The one is more a paraphrase of the other using similar wording, and the epigram does not come at quite the same place in both. There is no way of telling which is the earlier, but it can be said that between the text of Michigan 2754 and the Hadrianic *Contest* much the same process of paraphrase seems to be happening as is found between the narrative sections of the third century BC Flinders Petrie papyrus and the Hadrianic version.

It was argued by Kirk that ll.1–14 and ll.15–25 of the papyrus were separate texts which somehow arrived on the back of the same bill together, and Dodds, shortly after, accepted Kirk's argument. Koniaris took a rather different line but came to much the same conclusion. The case for this was questioned by West, and two rigorous and convincing analyses by Renehan have removed many of the arguments for separate texts. There is no doubt that ll. 15–25 represent a personal conclusion, and Dodds was surely right to point out that the end of the papyrus with the *subscriptio* is in the typical form of the end of a papyrus book with the author and title concluding the work. It seems therefore a very likely hypothesis that the papyrus text is a whole and contains the end of a book (or section of a book) about Homer by Alcidamas, and that this was used and 'adapted' by the compiler of the *Mouseion.* G.S. Kirk,'The Michigan Alcidamas–Papyrus; Heraclitus Fr.56D; the riddle of the lice', *CQ* 44 (1950), 149–67; E.R. Dodds, 'The Alcidamas–Papyrus again', *CQ* n.s.2 (1952), 187–8; G.L. Koniaris, 'Michigan Papyrus 2754 and the *Certamen*', *HSCP* 75 (1971), 107–29; M.L. West, 'The contest of Homer and Hesiod', *CQ* n.s.17 (1967), 433–50; R. Renehan, ' The Michigan Alcidamas–Papyrus: A Problem in Methodology', *HSCP* 75 (1971), 85–105;

id. Studies in Greek Texts(Göttingen,1975), 144–59.

φθειρίζεσθαι....φθειρῶν – for an exhaustive account of the body-louse and the many stories with which it was involved in antiquity, see M.Davies and J. Kathirithamby, *Greek Insects* (Oxford,1986), 169–76.

ποιεῖσθαι τὴν ἀρετήν – for ἀρετή with the sense of 'reputation for distinction', cf. Thuc. i.33 φέρουσα ἐς μὲν τοὺς πολλοὺς ἀρετήν.

παιδιᾶς – an interesting hint of changing attitudes to Homer and epic poetry: Homer is now becoming light entertainment, though he is still regarded an essential element in Greek culture (τοῖς βουλομένοις φιλοκαλεῖν τῶν Ἑλλήνων).

General Index

Agamemnon – *Od.* 21

Aleos, King of Tegea – *Od.* 14,15,16

Alexandros/Paris – *Od.* 7,17,18

archery – *OWS* 5; *Od.* 6

Archilochus – no.3

arrow – *Od.* 6–7

audience response – *OWS* 22–3

Auge – *Od.* 16

breastplate, gift to Agam. – *Od.* 21

Centaurs – *Od.* 23

Chilon – no.3

Chios – no.3

coinage – *Od.* 22–6

Crete – *Od.* 17,18

Cyprus – *Od.* 20

dice – *Od.* 22,27

Diomedes – *Od.* 5,7

Elaia – p. viii, xxvii

Elaites (Alcidamas) – p. ix

Elis – *Od.* 14

Eumolpos – *Od.* 23

Eurybates – *Od.* 6

fire-beacons – *Od.* 22,28

formations (for war) – *Od.* 22,23

Forms,theory of – *OWS* 27

Helen – *Od.* 17

Herakles – *Od.* 14,15,25

Homer – no.3, death of – no.27

Isthmian Games – no.15

javelin-throwing – *OWS* 5

Kinyras – *Od.* 20,21

Lapiths – *Od.* 23

lice – no.27

Linos – *Od.* 25

living speech – *OWS* 28

Lycurgus – no.4

memory – *OWS* 18–21

Menelaus – *Od.* 17,20

Menestheus – *Od.* 23

Molos,children of – *Od.* 17

Mousaios – *Od.* 25

music – *Od.* 22,25

Mysia – *Od.* 16

Nauplios – *Od.* 12,15

Nestor – *Od.* 23

Odyssey, mirror of life – no.25

Oiagros – *Od.* 24.

Oinopion – *Od.* 20

Orpheus – *Od.* 24

Palamedes – *Od. passim.*

Peirithoos – *Od.* 23

Polypoites – *Od.* 5

progress – *OWS* 26,32

runners – *OWS* 5

slavery – no.1

Sappho – no.3

Solon – no.4

Sthenelos – *Od.* 7

Telephos – *Od.* 7, 16, 17

Teukros – *Od.* 6, 8

Teuthras – *Od.* 16

water-clock – *OWS* 11

weight-lifting – *OWS* 5

weights and measures – *Od.* 22, 27

writing, discovery of – *Od.* 22, 24

Index of Greek words

ἄγραφος – *OWS* 24.
ἀγωνίζομαι – *OWS* 25,26.
αἰσχρός – *OWS* 18; *Od.* 8,21.
ἀκρίβεια – *OWS* 13,14,15,25,33.
  ἀκριβής – *OWS* 18.
  ἀκριβῶς – *OWS* 11,20,23,25,34.
ἀπορία – *OWS* 8,15,16,21.
  ἄπορος – *OWS* 17.
αὐτοσχεδιάζω – *OWS* 13,14,22,
  31,32,33,34.
αὐτοσχεδιασμός – *OWS* 18,20,23.
αὐτοσχεδιαστικός – *OWS* 8,29,
  30,33.
αὐτοσχεδιαστός – *OWS* 16,17.
βιβλίον – *OWS* 15,28.
γνώμη – *OWS* 6,8,9,12,16,17,18,
  23,34; *Od.* 1.
γράμμα – *Od.* 2,6,10,22,24.
γραμματεῖον – *OWS* 11.
γραπτός – *OWS* 1,14,18,25.
δεινός – *OWS* 6,15,34; *Od.* 4,26.
δηλόω – *OWS* 18,19,23; *Od.* 7,24,
  26.
δύναμις – *OWS* 1,2,6,7,9,10,15
  23,29,30,34; no.6.
εἰκῆ – *OWS* 25,29,33; *Od.* 1,8.
ἔμψυχος – *OWS* 28.
ἐνθύμημα – *OWS* 3,4,18,19,20,
  24,25,33.
εὐπόρημα – *OWS* 26.

εὐπορία – *OWS* 3.
εὔπορος – *OWS* 19,24,34.
  εὐπόρως – *OWS* 6,13.
καιρός – *OWS* 3,9,10,22,28,34;
  Od. 17
λογογράφος – *OWS* 6,13.
λογοποιός – *OWS* 8.
λόγος – *OWS* 1,3,8,10,11,13–16,
  18–21,23–25,27–31,32; *Od.* 1,
  12; no.9.
μνήμη – *OWS* 18,19,32,34.
ὄνομα – *OWS* 3,12,18,19,20,24,
  25,33,34; *Od.* 12.
ποιητής – *OWS* 2,34.
ῥῆμα – *OWS* 16,19.
σοφιστής – *OWS* 1,2,4;*Od.* 12,21.
τάξις – *OWS* 24,28,33; *Od.* 22,23.
φιλοσοφέω – *Od.* 12,22.
  φιλοσοφία – *OWS* 2,15,29;no.24
  φιλόσοφος – *Od.* 4; no.4.
χρόνος – *OWS* 4,8,10,15,17,21,
  31;*Od.* 6,9.
ψυχή – *OWS* 6,16,17,34; nos. 7,
  17,19,22.